The
Gudge Creek
and
Wad Chronicles

THE
GUDGE CREEK
AND
WAD CHRONICLES

For Walter Hussman
who makes life in Little Rock very
interesting

Richard Allin

Richard Allin

9.7.89

The University of Arkansas Press
Fayetteville   1989   London

DESIGNER: *Chang-hee H. Russell*
TYPEFACE: *Goudy Old Style*
TYPESETTER: *G & S Typesetters, Inc.*
PRINTER: *Thomson-Shore, Inc.*
BINDER: *John H. Dekker & Sons, Inc.*

Illustrations by David Allen Katley

The paper used in this publication meets the minimum requirements
of the American National Standard for Permanence of Paper for
Printed Library Materials Z39.48-1984. ∞

Library of Congress Cataloging-in-Publication Data

Allin, Richard.
    The Gudge Creek and Wad chronicles / Richard Allin.
        p.   cm.
      ISBN 1-55728-076-2.
      ISBN 1-55728-077-0 (pbk.)
      1. City and town life—Arkansas—Humor.
2. Arkansas—Social life and customs—Humor.
I. Title.
F415.A45   1989
976.7—dc19   88-26775
                                                    CIP

This book is for Carol

THE
GUDGE CREEK
AND
WAD CHRONICLES

The voters of the twin communities of Gudge Creek (pop. 10) and Wad (pop. 9) are gearing up for the Super Wednesday primary elections. As always the towns will vote one hundred percent right.

The towns share a precinct, and procedures are simple. Election costs are minimal since only one pencil is sharpened for use by the nineteen voters. Ballots are mimeographed in the parlor of Second Baptist Church, where the elections are held. And they are short because they contain only the names of the winning candidates.

Early on, it was found that nineteen votes were not enough to influence any major election. So the citizens devised a scheme of holding elections a day after regular elections. With state and national returns all in, citizens could benefit from hindsight.

"You'd be surprised how the towns benefit from this," State Representative Wallace Wad told me on his last visit to the capital city.

"Since the populations of both towns vote as one, and always for the winning candidate, we have been rewarded through the years." He cited a couple of examples: A scheme by the power company to build a major steam plant beside Gudge Creek was thwarted by grateful politicians.

If the power company had had its way, their plant would have ruined fishing in Gudge Creek by using all the water for steam, and both towns would have had to be relocated to make room for the coal pile.

A threat by the highway department to pave the road into town was averted by a thankful governor, thanks to the town's correct vote in preceding elections. Townspeople have fought a paved road for years.

"We've got it like we want it," Representative Wad declared. "We don't want more people, and the problems they would bring if they could get in."

Representative Wad sounded unusually sincere for a legislator.

"Just think," he went on, "we don't have to bus our children to school because everybody in town lives across the street from the school. Now we know that the federal judges don't like that arrangement, but nobody has sued.

"We don't have any trouble settling disputes between ourselves because they ain't any lawyers in town. There's no police force because there's no crime. There are no city planners because with just one street we don't have any intersections. Parking's not a problem because we've got only three cars, and only two of them run. We've got a carefully balanced economy with a variety of little businesses because we're not big enough to have a Wal-Mart. In short, we've got it like we want it because we vote right every time!"

Several local issues helped increase the size of the ballots in Gudge Creek and Wad. Among them:

* An ordinance that would make the office of marshal in both towns purely honorary. The measure would do away with provisions for a salary altogether and appropriate only enough money to buy a badge for whomever holds the honorary office. The measure passed without dissent. (As crime is nonexistent in both towns, the post of marshal, while provided for, was not immediately filled.)

* A measure to provide for the feeding of wildlife on the pond in Twin Cities Municipal Park. The measure failed by a unanimous vote. (Voters thought that the town goose could fend for himself.)

* A measure to appropriate 13 million dollars for a new convention center and sports arena at Gudge Creek Community College. The measure passed with no dissent.

* An initiated measure to provide public funds to buy the third volume of the World Book Encyclopedia for the college library.

The measure failed. (The first two volumes had been funded by initiated ordinances in previous general elections; however, antitax feeling led to the defeat of Volume G through J.)

* An initiated ordinance to prohibit any representative of the Army Engineers from ever setting foot in either town. Passed unanimously. (More votes were cast on this measure than there are total voters in either town.) The Engineers have long been eyeing the creek from which Gudge Creek takes its name, with the eye of building a 65 million dollar dam, power plant, and recreation area on it. The totally automated power plant would create no new jobs, and the new generating facility would mean a doubling of utility rates in towns close to the dam. The rising waters would cause relocation of both towns.

With the return of autumn, and the reopening of Gudge Creek Community College, Gudge Creek (pop. 10) and Wad (pop. 9) have taken on a bustling air.

The entire student body returned by one chartered bus from Mineshaft, Pennsylvania, creating a traffic tangle on the one and only street as they all got off with their bags.

With the exception of the female cheering squad, the entire college coincides exactly with the entire basketball team. It was recruited in toto when Mineshaft Community College closed for a short time after the president absconded with the funds (and his secretary) and sought a new life in the Bahamas.

The first activity for the year was a meeting of the faculty committee on curriculum to set the calendar for the coming year. They were presented, right off, with something of a problem. They were troubled with finding any time at all for class during basketball season. After they had pencilled in all the basketball games for the year, only three class days could be found in January, and four in February.

"We'll do what we can to accommodate the Athletic Department," President Brewster Lurton declared. "But in order to award degrees, we think that the student should have completed at least *some* class work."

Athletic Director Lester Poke disagreed. "Times have changed, Brewster," Poke said. "In the old days—long gone—boys used to come to school to attend class. They played athletics on the side—in their spare time—for *free*! In them days, the college faculty actually outnumbered the athletic faculty.

"Them days is over. Tax-supported colleges is for football and basketball. If they's some time left over—and there ain't no good TV program on—then them boys can go to class."

Poke reminded President Lurton that in the old days, worthy players were awarded "letters." "Now, if they go to—say—half a dozen classes a semester, the college can award them a 'letter' in education. Only, you can call it a degree."

It made sense to Lurton, and to the rest of the college faculty. They sat around the table nodding assent and agreement.

"There's just *one* thing, Lester," Lurton said. "Some of them boys can't read, only just their names, maybe. Don't you think we could have a class—maybe voluntary, on the weekend—to teach 'em how to hold a pencil, and which way is up on a book page?"

Lester shook his head patiently. "Brewster, we can do all that, all right. But I say let them boys enjoy their college education. One thing I learned in college is, don't overload. You *can* take too many hours, you know."

Lurton was turned back by Poke's logic. Poke, not insensitive to the point of view of the educators, saw he had them whipped. So he made—generously—an offer of concession.

"I'll tell you what I'll do, Lurton," Poke said, "when we go on our bus trips, I'll invite along the dean of remedial reading and spelling. She can stand in the bus and learn the boys their ABCs, and maybe a few sentences while we drive."

6

The faculty committee broke into a patter of applause. After all, Poke didn't have to do that. "It'd make me feel a whole lot better, Lester," Lurton said. "After all, they're gonna have to do *some* reading after they get out of college—at least if they're gonna know what television programs are on."

The faculty committee also was faced with a housing problem brought about by an unusual circumstance. The incoming freshman class would have to be housed in the basement of the gymnasium because of shortage of dormitory space. The problem arose because nobody passed last semester. Every senior was having to repeat the grade.

It made for a curious, yet strangely satisfying commencement exercise. The program went on as usual, with a long invocation, a flute solo, valedictory and salutatory orations, remarks by the chairman of the Board of Trustees, the president's address, and the benediction. Many thought it was one of the nicest. Except no degrees were awarded.

"We hope to see some improvement during the coming year," the president had said at one point.

The faculty committee met late into the afternoon. It looked, on the whole, like it was going to be a good year.

If there's anything unique about Gudge Creek (pop. 10) and its bedroom community, Wad (pop. 9), it's the fact that they have only one street between them.

One town begins where the other leaves off—or vice versa, depending on which way you are traveling.

For years, since the communities became interested in civic development, they had been moderately chagrined that with just the one street they had no intersection. And with no inter-section, they had no traffic-light system.

"I don't see," spoke up Wardell Vex, director of the Twin City Development Council, "how we can ever amount to any-thing without a traffic-light system."

The council authorized Vex to hire a consultant from the capital city to see what could be done. The consultant, it seems, had just retired from the capital city's own renowned traffic signal system. After he had recuperated a while at the Shady Rest Sanitarium, doctors pronounced him fit to be re-turned to society—"as long as he doesn't work more than two days a week." That's when he decided to become a traffic consultant.

After spending six months at the twin cities studying the situation, the consultant informed Vex that he was ready to make his report. There was a single stipulation: He was to re-ceive his paycheck—a modest five thousand dollars—before the envelope was opened.

"Cheap at the price," exulted Vex as he ripped open the en-velope containing the report. He didn't notice that the consul-tant dodged out of the door as he concentrated on clawing open the manila flap.

As the council waited breathlessly, Vex read the report aloud:

"We recommend that a traffic light be hung at the point the driveway of Second Baptist Church comes into the street."

The council burst into applause. The consultant had done the impossible—provided a traffic light on a one-street town. Vex was sent to the capital city to talk with its municipal traffic officials. Upon his return he reported that he had hired the same company that had installed the street light system in the capital.

"Of course, we won't need no computers—just yet," Vex said.

The only skeptic was Uncle Dave Hicks, the local bootlegger.

"We ain't got but three cars in town," Uncle Dave reminded the council, "and don't but two of them run—mine and the truck at the DX station. And since we ain't got but one street, I don't see no need for a traffic light."

"It ain't so much the immediate need," said Vex, justifying the expenditure for the traffic signals, "as it is the spirit of the thing. Who's gonna look at a town that ain't got no traffic signals?"

Experts from the capital city arrived and hung the new light. A dedication day was set.

Vex himself was chosen to throw the switch to put the new system into operation. The two operating vehicles of the town were then to drive up and down the main street, stopping and starting as the lights indicated. The combined population of the two towns was to stand by and admire the proceedings. Then a fried chicken lunch was to be held on the grounds of Second Baptist Church—or in the parlor in case it rained.

The day arrived. Rev. Lucious Grumbles, the pastor, said an invocation. State Representative Wallace Wad of Wad delivered an appreciation of traffic officials from the capital city coming all the way for so little pay.

Then Vex flipped the switch. Red (stop) indications were given on the main street, where both cars were. Green (go) was given to the Baptist Church parking lot, where there were no cars.

And that's the way it still is. The light is still stuck. A yellow truck has pulled up by the open white box on the nearby lamp post and technicians are dickering and tinkering with the timing mechanism.

Meanwhile, the town marshal has been called away from his duties to direct traffic until the light system is repaired.

The townspeople did not view the unexpected malfunction with disappointment. No matter that the traffic signal doesn't work right. The important thing is that they have one.

I was waiting at a street corner here in the capital city one day last week for a United Parcel Service truck to clear.

Suddenly, out of the truck door popped the head of State Representative Wad of Wad. He had just arrived for a meeting of the House Committee on Absentee Voting, of which he is vice chairman. Since there's no bus service in his area, he had to ship himself by UPS.

"They put a little sticker on me and insure me for a hundred dollars automatically," Wad had once told me. "Any evaluation over that I have to pay for."

Wad thanked the driver and signed his clipboard to attest that he had been properly delivered.

"UPS is a good way to travel even though we do make a lot of stops," Wad said. "In fact, it's our best way to travel over where I live." He said he killed time along the way by helping the driver dolly parcels into businesses. "He's an awful nice fellow. That's a good company, too. And I don't know what we'd do without them over in Wad and Gudge Creek."

Gudge Creek (pop. 10) and Wad (pop. 9) are separated only by an imaginary line. Indeed, they are very close in several ways. They share the same fire department, which is a garden hose at the DX station. And they have the same telephone service, which is a crank phone at the Gudge Creek General Store.

They are located in a low place on the banks of Gudge Creek and might be said to be off the beaten path. Their only connection with the highway is a pair of inclined ruts kept in repair by frequent use of the local bootlegger's delivery truck. All other town deliveries are made to the intersection of the ruts with the highway.

Representative Wad's committee meeting wasn't until two that afternoon so he suggested we take lunch together. I was delighted to join him, knowing I'd be brought up on the latest news about the legislature, and politics in general.

Inevitably, the conversation turned to national politics. I was interested in what his townsmen thought about presidential candidates.

"We are sick of them, to tell the truth," Wad said. "I don't know how grown men can get up and ventilate so many half-truths about themselves and each other and expect the sincere voter to believe they are telling the truth.

"We tried to have a Democratic caucus in our two towns but got so disgusted that everybody took a solemn oath not to vote for *anybody* who was currently running for president.

"It ain't worth tearing your community apart by falling out over that bunch. One thing we have managed to do in Wad and Gudge Creek is live in peace. And one minute of that caucus stuff forewarned us that we'd better drop it and go on about our bidness or there was gonna be a shootin' or worse."

Wad said he was lukewarm on the law requiring competency tests for teachers, although he did vote for it. "It ain't just right," he said. "But then we got an assistant coach at Wad High School who has to be read to so he can teach his civics honors course. That ain't right.

"And old Mrs. Cue, the history teacher, ain't read nothin' past Roosevelt's first term. And she still thinks that Amelia Earhart ain't took off yet."

I shook my head in wonderment. There *did* seem to be something lacking in the Wad school system.

"The public liberry got no reference books so the Gudge Creek and Wad school chirren have to use the Community College liberry to write their term papers, and they ain't nothin' there but two volumes of the 1923 World Book, plus some back numbers of *Southern Living* give to them for the bicentennial by the DAR at the county seat."

I picked up the lunch check over Representative Wad's protests and bade him goodby on the curb as he waved down a bus going to the state capitol.

———————————

Uncle Dave Hicks runs a distillery on the banks of Gudge Creek. His product has been well known in the area of the twin towns of Gudge Creek (pop. 10) and Wad (pop. 9) for years.

His profession has earned Uncle Dave a good living. And his own personal charities and general good citizenship have given him a place of honor in local and county society.

If his profession is technically illegal, in the nicest sense of the word, it is a technicality that is overlooked, for Uncle Dave has been so generous in his contributions that there is no person in the county who has not been favorably affected.

A few days ago, Uncle Dave was asked to visit the state capital for a discussion with energy and transportation officials. It seems that the product of his distilling house is a liquid of such spirit that it can be used to power internal combustion engines.

Many consider it remarkable that the same carefully made liquid that is sipped to such benefit by townspeople when they have the rheum, the grippe, and the catarrh is identical to that poured into fuel tanks of the local car and truck that Uncle Dave services. If there is a fault with the product, it is that it is too strong, driving vehicles up to forty-five miles an hour in first gear.

Over at Gudge Creek Community College, administration officials decided at the outset of the second semester to create a full-fledged Department of Chemistry. Heretofore, a few basic chemistry courses had been offered by the Department of Home

Economics, among them, Chem. 104: *Why Baking Powder Rises,* MWF, Miss Digley; and Chem. 202: *The History of Heartburn,* TTS, Mr. Foxe-Waxman.

Until early last month budgetary conditions had made it impossible to expand the curriculum. It was then that the entire athletic department, along with all the basketball players, were indicted in a scandal that came to light when an Internal Revenue Service agent asked one of the coaches to sign his name. Subsequent tests showed that not a single member of the coaching staff, nor any member of the team, could either read or write.

This would not have been considered unusual under normal athletic circumstances, until investigators questioned the straight "A" transcripts of every member of the team, including "Jojo" the bullfrog, the team's official mascot. It turned out that Jojo's vital statistics had been entered into the computer by mistake. He was described as "green male, 17 ounces, age 2 years. Major: Mayfly culture."

The result was that the entire athletic program was canceled for the second semester, owing to the fact that everybody was in jail. That left the budgeted funds available for other purposes. The addition of a chemistry department was decided upon.

Uncle Dave Hicks' reputation as a chemist—largely self-taught—attracted the administration's attention, and he was asked if he would become temporary professor of chemistry and department head.

"Well, I'll tell you what," Uncle Dave responded to college president, Dr. Brewster Lurton, "I'll teach 'em what I can."

He explained that he would prefer to conduct his lectures in his own distillery house, and Dr. Lurton agreed.

It was also agreed that the college would confer a Ph.D. on Uncle Dave in order to maintain its high academic standards.

Did Uncle Dave have any preference in textbooks?

"No, sir. There ain't a whole lot that's wrote down on what I'm going to learn them."

"Well, Dr. Hicks," Dr. Lurton said, "I wish you'd jot down a syllabus so that we can have it printed in our catalogue."

After discussion with the university printer, the course outline read as follows:

Chem. 101: *Philosophy of Mash*; Chem. 201: *Epistemology of Yeasts and Sugars*; Chem. 324: *Probability of Proofs*; Chem. 387: *Theory of Distilling*; Chem. 521: *Bottling and Marketing.*

Lectures begin soon.

―――――――――

The cooperative spirit between the twin communities of Gudge Creek (pop. 10) and Wad (pop. 9) has always been healthy. Indeed, many visitors to one of the towns are unaware when they cross into the other, so faint are the barriers.

The Gudge Creek General Store, for example, serves both towns equally, there not being such a mercantile center in Wad. Then the Boat Dock Cafe at Wad is the principal eating establishment of the towns. Gudge Creek Community College is theoretically located in Gudge Creek although the road leading to it is in Wad. Hence a feeling of proprietary interest in both towns.

The Twin City Country Club has long represented the social integration of the towns. It is located across the creek and is reached by the community jon boat, which is tethered on an overhead line. The one-hole golf course is maintained by assessment of the members of both towns, as is the community golf bag and balls. Owing to the small size of the towns, the golf course is necessarily small. And its smallness, in turn, makes it feasible for a single golf bag—kept at the club house—to serve the membership.

Tennis is not allowed. It had been tried early in the century, but its pursuit so threatened family units that the grassy court was cultivated into mustard greens.

Each town has its own library building, maintained by a mill-age tax. The book collection, however, is kept in common and is moved back and forth between the towns on alternate weeks. Pride of the libraries are the *Reader's Digest* condensation of *The Robe, Aunt Ruth's Bible Stories* (edited for modern readers), and the *Poems of James Whitcomb Riley*.

The Twin City Community Concert Series maintains a collection of half a dozen phonograph records in the parlor of Second Baptist Church, which owns a gramophone, and a spring and fall series of programs are enjoyed. Recently a committee with representatives from both towns was appointed to secure a new record.

Almost from the first the Twin City Fire Department has served both towns. Indeed, the fire department is unique in the annals of fire fighting. It consists of a spigot located in the side of the DX station, with a hose long enough to reach every structure in both towns.

As for the police department, a town marshal serves each town every other day, in an honorary position. Crime being nonexistent in Gudge Creek and Wad, no one ever locks doors. The Pepsi-Cola box at the DX station is on the honor system.

Even with the examples of cooperation between Gudge Creek and Wad there has never been any serious thought of a merger. "Both towns would just rather remain of a manageable size," commented State Representative Wallace Wad of Wad. "Merger would only be a step toward megalopolis. And large size does not necessarily bring a heightened quality of life." So, even though it means maintaining two city governments, the feeling is that two towns (pop. 10 and pop. 9) are better than one larger town (pop. 19).

"After all, as close as we are," said Mrs. Vernelle Inch of Gudge Creek, "we do have our own traditions and customs."

It was in this spirit that a fifteen-member committee came into existence to explore other methods by which the towns could cooperate in the name of friendship and economy. Gudge

Creek, the larger of the towns, was given the extra member of the committee.

The meeting was held in the faculty lounge of Gudge Creek Community College, next to the basketball inflating room.

"I swow," said Wardell Vex, scratching his head after the session had been in progress fifteen minutes, "I just don't see what else we can do. If we want to cooperate any more, we'll have to undo something so we can do it again."

Everybody nodded. There was a motion that, since everything was moot, the meeting be adjourned *sine die.* It would let the committee stay in existence to find ways to cooperate in anything unforeseen that might arise.

―――――――――

The faculty and staff of Gudge Creek Community College were back in place last week preparing for the upcoming academic semester.

"We're still struggling with devising an academic program for our athletic department," Vice President Lurton Soames told department heads, "but otherwise the course of study for the coming year has been set."

"We are going to be able to offer advanced chemistry once again," Mr. Soames said happily, "thanks to the return to the department of Dr. David L. Hicks."

Uncle Dave Hicks, as he is better known in the twin communities of Gudge Creek (pop. 10) and Wad (pop. 9), has decided to resume his teaching career.

"Some of his business interests," Vice President Soames explained, "have been turned over to his sons, Jack Daniels Hicks and James Beam Hicks."

Uncle Dave has for years been the chief benefactor, booster, and guiding light for the two towns, and for the college to which he has given so much time and money.

"And thanks to income realized from our endowment, the library has been able to buy a third volume of the World Book encyclopedia—G through J—making it possible to add additional majors to our college catalogue."

Mr. Soames also announced that the home economics department will be able to add a freshman course in Basic Meatloaf.

"Still, the athletic department is presenting us with some thorny problems. As it now stands, their only required course is Sunday School, taught by the coaching staff and members of the department of athletics."

"Yes, but is that really enough of a college course?" the chairman of the history department asked. "Don't we owe them something else?"

"Well, there has never been a strong connection between academics and athletics in tax-supported institutions of higher learning," Mr. Soames answered. "Still, improvements are possible."

"I'd like to suggest that all be required to take a basic biology course," the science chairman said.

"A good idea, Miss Bemley, but I've been informed by the assistant coach that any mention of Darwinian evolution would be against the will of God, as far as the athletic department is concerned."

"Well, we could skip over the monkeys. Anything would be more than they're getting now."

"We'll take it under advisement, Miss Bemley," Mr. Soames said. "Now, are there any other comments?"

Just then Uncle Dave Hicks hove through the door and sat down near the front table. "Professor Hicks, have you anything to say?"

"I say let's cut the sham. Forget academic subjects for athletes. Could any of you pay attention Monday after being squashed on Saturday?

"And how do you expect some poor feller who couldn't read

a McDonald's menu in high school to play basketball four nights a week in four different towns and then graduate from college?

"I say let's cut the make-believe. Let's just pay 'em a salary to play as our team and stop pretending that they are in college."

"Now, now, Dr. Hicks. That is perhaps a bit too progressive to be considered just now."

"You're danged right it is. (Chuckle.) I just wanted to watch you all squirm in your seats a little bit. Now, let's vote to keep on doing what we been doing. It don't make everybody happy. But it durn near comes close."

State Representative Wallace Wad, of Wad, was in town one day last week, and he brought me up to date on recent happenings in the twin cities of Gudge Creek (pop. 10) and its bedroom community, Wad (pop. 9).

"I had wanted to come in last month," Representative Wad said over a cup of Postum at the bus station cafe, "but the weather was just too much." For the first time in a century petrolacutation had failed because of a rare conjunction of the planets, and both towns were in shock.

He reported how the ruts leading from the highway down into the twin communities had iced up and it was impossible to get a pickup truck up them.

"We got our regular deliveries, all right," he said. "They'd put stuff in a box on the upper end, and it'd just slide right down. We was thankful for *that.*"

He said that because of the severe cold that Gudge Creek Community College had to cancel remedial reading and pre-arithmetic classes. "Since they could keep only one building heated," Wad said, "they chose the gymnasium so as not to interrupt the basketball schedule." Fortunately, he pointed out, the college administrative offices are located in a cubicle off the gymnasium boiler room, so the president could stay at his desk.

Snow and ice conditions caused severe hardships on the twin communities, but the populace met the challenge. An example, said Representative Wad, was when an accumulation of ice caused the streamer with the green-on-green pennants at the DX station to snap under the weight. This streamer has long been a point of pride in Gudge Creek, proudly strung from the top of the sign—the tallest structure in town—to the corner of the metal awning in front of the building.

The very afternoon that the streamer snapped, a public subscription was mounted to have it repaired and restrung.

Street damage in both communities was extensive, and it put a strain on the road repair equipment which consisted entirely of a retired railroad coal shovel and a five-pound box of ice cream salt. (The salt was transferred from the Twin City Parks Department, where it was declared surplus from previous Independence Day activities.)

Hard as times were, the fact that Representative Wad had made it out to the highway to catch the bus to the capital city was evidence that the weather had moderated and the icebound ruts had thawed enough to permit at least foot passage.

Representative Wad said his purpose for coming to town was to consult with an architectural firm which had designed the Township-Centre Mall for Gudge Creek.

Gudge Creek, always forward looking, never misses an opportunity to copy the best features of its larger neighbors. The city board voted to turn the town's only street into a pedestrian mall to revitalize the area and make it more pleasant for shoppers.

Gudge Creek doesn't really have a street of its own, just a flat place where the ruts from the highway sort of level out. And it's only a storefront long until it's back out in the country.

Nevertheless, the community voted a bond issue, a design was made, work was begun and it was finished in one day. The next day the only store on it announced that it was closing.

But it did spruce up downtown. A concrete planter with a plastic crape myrtle tree was brought in and tastefully placed across the road from the defunct store. Its placement was the only real engineering problem that workmen met. They were forced to cut down a dozen wild dogwood trees which stood in the way.

The planter has a dual purpose. It also serves as a rubbish receptacle.

Representative Wad said the closing of the town's only store was unexpected, and he needed to consult with the architects to see if they had any other crowd-pleasing ideas that might bring people to the area.

We both finished our Postum, and as we parted I invited him to call me again when he came to town.

Should the ability to read and write be an entrance requirement to Gudge Creek Community College?

That's the issue faced by the Admissions Committee for this fall.

"We're darned if we do and we're darned if we don't," said Dr. Brewster Lurton, GCCC president.

"I mean," Dr. Lurton asked, "are reading and writing meaningful to life, and therefore a prerequisite for a modern college? Gudge Creek Community College is facing a dilemma.

"High schools are graduating more and more students who can neither read nor write. Yet, without a college diploma, these people will be marked for life. Is it fair not to admit them to college? Can they expect to compete in the outside world without a college degree?"

"Certainly not in this day and time when a good education means everything." The speaker was the dean of the college of arts and sciences.

"Frankly," Dr. Lurton added, "some college courses have simply been too hard. It's time that we tailored our courses to the real needs of our students."

"You are right, sir," Coach Fabius Still said. "I have learned over the years that such character-building activities as collegiate basketball don't depend upon a player's ability to read and write."

(Nod of assent.)

"Well, perhaps we can make literacy optional," suggested Dr. Vanelda Davenport, head of the English department. "It doesn't hurt, you know, for literature majors to have at least a basic knowledge of reading and writing."

"A charming, if rather old-fashioned idea," Coach Still chuckled amiably. "We do have talking books, you know."

"Indeed we do," Dr. Davenport responded, "but as yet with only *Treasure Island* and two years of *Reader's Digest* condensations on tape we are not strong enough to offer a good solid major in English literature for the student who has decided, for his own reasons, not to learn to read."

"Well, we certainly can't be too choosy," the business manager, Jimmy Dee Dander, commented. "Colleges are having to compete for students. And since public-supported high schools are no longer making literacy a graduation requirement, I don't see why we should be so high-falutin' about it."

"Frankly," Coach Still broke in, "I prefer a totally illiterate boy, six-foot-eight, with enough finger spread to pick up a basketball with one hand. A kid who can't read don't have so much to unlearn."

The meeting lasted until late in the afternoon before a consensus was reached. As it stood, the college would accept any student from any accredited high school who came with a diploma of graduation. No questions regarding the ability to read or write would be asked.

Secondly, it was agreed that no student would be allowed to fail any course for reasons stemming from an inability to read and write.

———————

Uncle Dave Hicks has always been a good citizen. He has lived a quiet, productive life, respected by the citizens of Gudge Creek (pop. 10) and Wad (pop. 9) whom he had served more than half a century.

But the press of times put a strain on Uncle Dave. He had to decide whether to continue his tranquil life of quiet service or thrust his talents into the marketplace. The Twin City Development Council wanted him to take the latter course. The thoughtful citizens of the town wanted him to continue the former.

For half a century Uncle Dave had provided the towns with what they would otherwise have done without, or could have had only at enormous expense. Gudge Creek and Wad were officially "dry" (except for 3.2 beer), a condition inflicted upon themselves in 1917 when the young men were away and could not vote.

Uncle Dave, then a younger man, had immediately stepped forward to fill the gap. And as the years passed and the youths who had gone to war returned, there was never any question of voting the towns wet again. It was a tribute to Uncle Dave, a true craftsman, who made a much better product than was available in legal stores, and who sold it for much less.

Uncle Dave bought grains locally and contracted for the best charcoal for his filtering process, which kept a small local industry alive. He trained local boys as technicians to operate his distillery in the neat building by the creek, and did a fine job teaching chemistry at the Community College. He had no formal education beyond six years in a one-room school, but Uncle Dave knew all there was about the boiling point of alcohol and that of water.

Uncle Dave, a natural philosopher, never thought of himself as breaking the law. He reasoned that if God devised a system that made it natural for yeast to convert sugar to alcohol, then it was his duty to make the best of God's system. He developed this humane philosophy as a youth after observing how a jug of grape juice set aside by his mother for jelly making had been turned into wine by simply being let alone. This had been done by nature. And it would take a negative act of man to kill the process. That simple observation of natural law had been enough for Uncle Dave. Man, he reasoned, has no right to fiddle with nature, or to refuse nature's gifts.

The result of Uncle Dave's philosophy was a dark golden

liquid that issued forth from charred white oak barrels that had been held at least six years in his private warehouse.

His product was never misused in the twin towns. Many considered it medicinal. Because of Uncle Dave, it had never been necessary to try to attract a physician to minister to the town.

Then came the national fuel crunch and the talk of "gasohol." Wardell Vex, executive director of the Twin City Development Council, saw Uncle Dave's distillery as a hometown promoter's dream. He and a select committee went to Uncle Dave to propose that he stop his production of his traditional product and turn his resources to distilling alcohol for fuel for outsiders, too.

"Listen, Hicks," enthused Vex, "It'll put Wad and Gudge Creek on the map. We'll become the gasohol capital of the state!" Vex was getting carried away. He saw the development of a petro-alcohol-chemical complex developing right there in the twin cities, using Uncle Dave's production facilities as a beginning.

Uncle Dave thought for a while before he spoke. "Wardell," he began, pausing to remove a cud of chewing tobacco from his cheek so as better to articulate, "the trouble with the world now is we got too dang many promoters like you around. I'll bet you'd grow hay on your grandpaw's grave if you could make a dime out of it."

Wardell didn't proceed. He had been put in his place, and the twin cities had been spared industrialization.

Uncle Dave walked back to his distillery, conscious that the sun was shining as pretty as it ever did, the birds were singing as happy as ever, with the trees dappling shade around over the grass.

Back at his office, Uncle Dave called his staff together, poured them all a good glass of Uncle Dave's Best, and then gave them the rest of the day off.

Every now and then the newspapers will carry an item about a wine or beer license being denied a new restaurant because it's located too close to a church or school house.

These denials are precautionary, as we understand it. The arbitrary distance—two or three hundred feet—is the distance beyond which one cannot hurl an empty beer bottle after it's been emptied at the restaurant table. The rule is designed to protect stained glass windows, in the case of churches, and to prevent broken bottles in the playgrounds, in the case of schools.

But it was only recently that a unique situation arose in the town of Wad (pop. 9). A small tavern has been located at Wad for more years than present day residents can remember. It has been known for the peace of its deportment. It is solely for the refreshment and relaxation of local residents, strangers being subtly discouraged. Besides offering a locally brewed beer, the tavern also serves local cheeses, pickles, and homemade bread.

So quiet is its operation that the existence of the tavern is little known outside the town of Wad. Some of the population of neighboring Gudge Creek (pop. 10) are unaware of its existence, even though it has been there more than three-quarters of a century. Both students and faculty of Gudge Creek Community College, a few hundred feet away from the tavern, are forbidden from using the tavern.

"Call it discrimination if you want," commented publican Lester Cue, "but there are just some people we don't want."

Recently, missionaries from a church in the county seat held a camp meeting in a pasture on the outskirts of Wad, and, as the response was friendly, it was planned that a new church would be built inside the town limits.

That is, until it was learned that the church would be located within seventy-five feet of the Wad tavern.

"That just wouldn't do," said Cue in an interview at the courthouse in the county seat. "We had to get an injunction to stop it."

A delegation from Wad testified before the chancery judge at the county seat that the peaceful demeanor of the tavern should not be threatened or disturbed as would be the case in the close proximity of a new church.

Members of the delegation argued that "traffic at all hours of day and night; a raised noise level during the traditional quiet hours, especially on Sundays and Wednesdays; and the comings and goings of persons hostile to the peaceful operation of a tavern would create an intolerable situation and alter the nature of a peaceful business that has operated in the same place for the better part of a century."

The chancellor, citing ample precedence and current rules of the state Alcohol Beverage Control authority, ruled that the building of a church so close to the tavern was clearly illegal and against the best interest of the community.

Well, I guess it was bound to happen sooner or later. There are few things that can more upset the routine of a tavern than to have church members taking up all the parking spaces.

I happened to run across State Representative Wallace Wad of Wad a couple of days ago. He had come to the capital city on business, traveling as usual with the UPS man.

"We didn't celebrate winning our lawsuit or nothing," Representative Wad said. "That wouldn't have been right. We *did* invite the missionaries over for a beer, but only two or three accepted. We had a real nice visit."

State Representative Wallace Wad holds positions of authority in the state legislature, but he is, before all, a businessman. Last week he returned home on business he felt could lead to riches.

Wad (pop. 9) and its neighbor, Gudge Creek (pop. 10), have never let their size keep them from enjoying finer things. Representative Wad is owner and operator of the local boat dock, and the owner (but not operator) of the adjoining cafe, which is run by his sister, Mrs. Foster Cue.

Travel broadens. It was no time at all after Representative Wad came to the capital city for legislative meetings that he started frequenting the better eating places.

The capital city had a-plenty. For one month, Representative Wad dined out every night in a different place and never left the same street.

He started at one end and has still not reached the other. Some of his favorites were Cap'n D's, Kentucky Fried Chicken, Mr. Gatti's, McDonald's, Bongo Burger, Burger Chef, Burger King, Taco Tico, Tico Taco, Taco Taco, Tico Tico, Tak-a-Tako, Taco Kid, Taco Bell, Wendy's, Danver's, Pizza Hut, Pizza Inn, Pizza Planet, Shakey's Pizza, Ken's Pizza, Minute Man, Long John Silver's, Sambo's, Sonic, Sweden Creme, Dairy Queen, Sizzlin' Steak, and Chicken Country, to name a couple.

Representative Wad, something of a known trencherman in his own community, was ecstatic with the choices.

This concentration of eating establishments, all of which appeared to make a million dollars a day, put an idea into his mind. And he boarded the UPS van at the capital city for the ride home where he would put his idea into reality.

Representative Wad had determined to bring modern up-to-date food service to Wad and Gudge Creek. He felt, as the

town's only restaurant owner, the responsibility to provide the best for his communities.

He was to meet with a promotion and sales representative of the national quickie chain, Pizza Hovels, Inc. Pizza Hovel was well known to him. He had appreciated their patriotic gesture in planning a Pizza Hovel in the capital city, directly across the street from the city's most sacred park, next to the Chapel of Waffles (which served breakfast twenty-four hours a day in a religious motif).

As he rode homeward, he mused with pleasant enthusiasm what a new plastic red roof, plastic walls, plastic windows, plastic chairs, plastic tables, and paper plates would do to perk up what he realized was a sort of drab community, love it though he did.

He had pleasant visions of the townspeople sitting down to freshly thawed and baked anchovy-and-sausage pizzas with vanilla shakes, followed by succulent chocolate marshmallow dessert pizzas.

He also reckoned that modern preparation methods would allow him to reduce the number of workers in his own cafe (which had recently skyrocketed to two because of increasing demand for the food).

Mrs. Cue could stay on to operate the thawer and the electric pizza oven.

As it is, Mrs. Cue—who knew no better—operated her cafe on inefficient old-fashioned methods. Her backwardness as a cook was reflected in the menu which she chalked up each day on a blackboard: Fried Chicken with Gravy, Pork Roast with Apples, Turkey and Dressing, Smothered Pork Chops with Mashed Potatoes, Baked Steak, Brown Beef Stew, Chicken and Dumplings, and Center Cut Ham Steak with Pineapple, to name a few.

She also insisted on the hopelessly rural practice of accompanying the above items with fourteen different fresh vegetables, all from her garden. Of the "either" kinds of pies she served, five were of fruits from her orchard. The Lemon Ice Box Pie came through courtesy of Eagle Brand condensed milk.

Representative Wad reasoned that the land wasted on the vegetable garden and the orchard could be turned into a parking lot, perhaps even a *paved* parking lot. "After all," he thought as the van neared his stop, "pizza is bound to be a big seller, especially with our young people."

The van steamed off down the highway after it left him at the dirt road down to the twin communities. Representative Wad walked briskly toward a new beginning.

———————

As the heat of the summer rises, my thoughts wander off to those two towns that nature blessed so sweetly—Gudge Creek (pop. 10) and Wad (pop. 9).

Blessed because of a natural phenomenon. The actual temperature in the two towns remains at exactly seventy-two degrees Fahrenheit, winter and summer, day and night, every day of the year. It is a condition, to be explained below, that obtains only in those two communities, making them unique on the globe.

I asked State Representative Wallace Wad of Wad why the two towns never seemed to grow.

"Well, we know what we've got here." Wad said. "We just don't want no more people."

The odd weather phenomenon is created by a process called "petrolacutation," a process that results from the interaction of the coolness of the water in Gudge Creek and the warmth of the sun-bathed limestone beside the stream.

"The Engineers come out here to investigate us, and we held a meeting at the school house. They said it was a condition that ought to be looked into, and that a dam might be advisable."

At that time, the Engineers hadn't used up their appropriations and were looking for something to spend it on.

"It sounded like a good idea," Wad said, "except that a dam would raise the level of the creek to such an extent that both towns would have to be relocated to higher ground." It would put them outside the blessed area.

"We was polite about it, but Uncle Dave Hicks explained to them if they didn't get out of town, they would be responsible for their own safety.

"The Engineers didn't take to our hospitality all that much," Wad said. "Uncle Dave was a mite strident as he was running them out of town. The colonel shouted back over his shoulder that they could make us do it if we wasn't careful, and that we'd better watch out."

Representative Wad said that the towns were so careful about controlling their population that they had their own immigration service. "We ask that local families try not to entertain visitors and relatives at the same time. It just puts too much pressure on our facilities."

During my conversations with Wad, I'm always impressed about how much sense their policies make. "We know what we kin do and what we cain't."

"We're still a-scared of them Engineers," he said, shaking his head. "When they got money left over, they *got* to spend it somewhere. We don't welcome them in to town, but they're making airplane flights over us making photographs. That means they are serious about damming the creek."

Interest by the Engineers is not the first time the towns have been troubled by the promise of progress. The Power and Light Company had once wanted to put a coal-fired generating plant there.

"Uncle Dave run them off, too," Wad said. "It would have helped our tax situation; it is true. But they wanted to put the coal pile where the two towns are. And we didn't want to move."

He said it would have destroyed the fishing because the steam plant would daily evaporate all the water in Gudge Creek.

It would have made petrolacutation impossible. Summer temperature would have risen to ninety-eight degrees.

"As it is now, nobody don't even have heaters and air conditioners in either town.'

I always enjoy talking to Wad about the two towns, as our own temperature hovers at one hundred degrees. For liveability, the two towns can't be faulted. The residents seem to realize that.

A generous bequest of seventy-eight dollars from a former resident of Gudge Creek (pop. 10) made it possible for Gudge Creek Community College to expand the library.

The money was "earmarked" in the will, meaning it must be used only to purchase books—and nothing else.

The college faculty, rather than lose the money, decided that they might as well go ahead and stock the library.

It did not please all. Coach Fabius Still, pointing to a dire need to re-stripe the floor of the gymnasium, urged that the administration go to court to try to break the will so that the money could be freed for more worthwhile projects.

"Old folks who leave money are often not in their right minds," Coach Still told the faculty meeting. "I feel that he or she was perhaps befuddled in the mind. No chancery judge would force us to divert such useful funds from more pressing problems."

"Don't let no goldurned lawyers get aholt of this matter," Uncle Dave Hicks warned. "They won't be enough left to buy a Big Chief tablet with."

Coach Still was disturbed. "Dave," he said, "The liberry just ain't high on our list of priorities."

34

"You needn't fret, Fabius," broke in Uncle Dave. "We ain't gonna tarnish our image *too* much by buying seventy-eight dollars worth of books for the liberry."

"Well, just where are we gonna *put* 'em when we *get* 'em?" Fabius asked.

"Well, we could put 'em in the boys' cloakroom. They's a little shelf at one end where the janitor keeps his can of floorsweep."

Coach Still was overruled nine to eight by the faculty and the discussion turned to the next step—a deeply serious subject.

"What books are we gonna buy?" asked Miss Fostoria Foscue, associate professor of reading.

"Better decide *first* what we *don't* want to buy," intoned Dr. Zerble Swint, professor of remedial religion. "There's much *much* tr-o-o-o-th to be de-e-e-fended." Dr. Swint had a way with vowels, a course he minored in at seminary. "We must needs weed out the nutritionless *cha-a-aff* lest the *se-e-ed corn* be contaminated."

The room, awed by his organ tones, remained silent waiting for him to continue. He did.

"For example," Dr. Swint began, "we must prohibit *a-a-all* the words of Mark Twain, on the ground that he was a whiskey-swilling, cigar-smoking, profanity-spouting, preacher-hating *he-e-eathen*." Dr. Swint's fist hit the table on the last word.

Uncle Dave let out a rumbling chuckle. "Gad, Zerble. He don't sound half bad."

"He's roastin' in the B-a-a-a-d Place, cast there by an a-angry Gawd," Dr. Swint roared.

"By dogies," said Uncle Dave softly, "If Twain's in hell, I'm gonna give it another chance." Dr. Swint didn't hear.

"All the works of Darwin will be pro-o-ohibited for obvious reasons," Dr. Swint continued his list. "The works of Shakespeare and Marlowe because . . . well they're just *not* the type men I'd want my family to asso-o-ociate with."

Uncle Dave raised his hand. "I believe, Zerble, that we ought to make a *general* rule about the books we buy. Let's just say that we'll not buy *any* book that has *anything* about drinkin', cussin', sex, hell-raisin', fightin', killin', torture, child molestin', witchcraft, idolatry, stealin', sabbath-breakin', gamblin', and so forth."

Dr. Swint clearly warmed to Uncle Dave's apparent wisdom. "Dave," he said forthrightly, "You have shown g-r-e-a-t-t wisdom. Yes, you are exactly right. If we can keep from our liberry those books that have those horrid subjects mentioned, we'll do well in spreading the tr-o-o-o-th and the way and the light."

Uncle Dave, crusty to the last, sprung his trap.

"Swint, you pious noodle!" guffawed Uncle Dave. "We just outlawed the Holy Bible and *Webster's Unabridged Dictionary.*"

GCCC president, Brewster Lurton, seeing an uncomfortable situation developing, gaveled the meeting to a close.

The faculty members rose and filed out of the room, conferring as they walked in small groups. There was a suggestion in their demeanor that even though the majority favored expansion of the library, members of the minority had projects in mind that they considered more important. Among the most vocal was Coach Still who couldn't understand how rational people could be a party to such waste.

Gudge Creek (pop. 10) is hardly ever without a civic project of some sort.

Over the years, civic energy has resulted in smoothing out the ruts leading into town, acquisition of a community college—complete with a basketball team—after a northern community college went bankrupt, and establishment of a college music department when the Methodist Church at the county seat donated an old piano.

Each acquisition was recognized by one of Gudge Creek's

unique parades. The town's main street is so short that a committee decorates a stationary trailer in front of the general store to look like a float. Townspeople walk by it as the Victrola in the parlor of the Second Baptist Church plays marches.

A recent project was the expansion of the fire department that Gudge Creek shares with neighboring Wad (pop. 9). Enough money was raised at a Fireman's Ball to buy another length of garden hose. Getting the volunteer firemen together is a simple matter of the DX station operator banging the rim of a truck tire with a lug wrench. He then runs and attaches the hose to the hydrant, turns it on, and runs the nozzle to the fire.

Town and gown cooperate remarkably well, and during one summer a cake walk was held at the college gymnasium to raise funds to buy spellers for the English department. Future plans call for the offering of a Bachelor of Science in Education in spelling and penmanship.

So the townspeople took it in stride when it was announced at a Twin City Development Council meeting that the next project should be to get a seven-thousand-seat sports arena.

"We think that we are preparing for the future," Wardell Vex, executive director of the council, said. "It will take care of our athletic and convention needs for years to come."

The plan called for the arena to be constructed at considerable savings. No contract would be let, as the labor would be largely volunteer from the manual training class of Gudge Creek High School. They would use scrap lumber that accumulated over the years during rises in the Gudge Creek.

The "fabric" cover for the arena would come from a revival tent left over from a crusade of Brother Cashel Pipkin, whose evangelistic efforts came to an end when his first wife, whom he had overlooked divorcing, showed up with county officers.

The tent would be stretched—over homemade bleachers—from used utility poles.

The sports arena is both a popular and controversial question in Gudge Creek and neighboring Wad. "We so wanted an elevator in town," complained Mrs. Vernelle Inch, who had experienced the thrill of elevator rides on visits to the capital city.

Her suggestion was overruled when it was pointed out that neither Gudge Creek nor Wad had a building of more than one story.

"Well, we'll grow," Mrs. Inch protested, "and we might as well prepare for it."

It was not clear as to how the sports arena would be used. The student body of Gudge Creek High School totals only four—one short of a team.

And while Gudge Creek Community College supports a basketball team, college rules forbid playing on a dirt floor. The first spectacle suggested for the arena was a civic club "minstrel" to be imported from the county seat.

Vex was undismayed. "We can't be a first class town unless we act like one," he said.

A faculty committee appointed by the president of Gudge Creek Community College to choose meaningful names for the various buildings, formal rooms, scenic walks, and quadrangles at the college pondered briefly last Wednesday before turning in its report.

"Some may think that the names we applied lack imagination and verve," said a committee member. "But we are following the lead of the tastemakers in the capital city who have had much more experience at this than we."

Thus the main building at the college will now be known as "Main Building." The new multimillion dollar gymnasium, donated by the parents of a student, will be called, "College Gymnasium."

A plaque near the ceremonial front door will read, in bronze, "Front Door." The new student union building will be called

"Coffee And Shoppe," the latter "pe" added to "shop" to make it "dressier."

The quadrangle with the statue of the founder of Gudge Creek Community College will be known as "Please Use Walkways."

The membership of the committee had originally chosen names more representative of an educational institution. The main building was to be known as "King's College First," the gymnasium was to have been called "Circus Maximus Secundus," and the student union building was to be called "The Scholars' Common."

The huge heroic statue of Dr. Ezekiel Gudge was to have been surrounded by a grassy quadrangle known as "Founder's Quad."

But wiser minds won out, observed Dr. Zerble Swint, professor of remedial religion at the college, the committee chairman. "This way we won't hurt anybody's feelings in perpetuity."

This change of heart, it was disclosed after the committee turned in its report, occurred after Dr. Swint paid a visit to the state capital and noted a similar action taken there.

"That board," Dr. Swint told his colleagues, "is made up of members of only the highest ideals, widest vision, boldest imagination. Without these characteristics you don't get elected to such an important post in a big place like the capital city."

It was quite coincidental with Dr. Swint's visit that the capital city Board of Directors approved a list of names for its own new convention center, its rooms, and areas.

The Board had appointed a blue ribbon committee of the richest, smartest, and foremost citizens to come up with a list of names. They returned a veritable poetry of names: "State House Center," for the overall complex. Meeting rooms in the center are to be called such rose-colored whoppers as "Chamber Room," "State Room," and "Council Room." There's also to be a "Governor's Exhibition Hall," although it was not explained just what the governor was to have to do with it.

When the list was presented to the capital city Board of Directors, the members applauded, moaned, sighed, and wept at the beauty. They immediately approved the list, noting that there was no opposition to it.

One of the star board members noted that it was better to stay with the more *general* type name so that feelings would not be hurt, toes not trod upon, nor luminaries overlooked.

"Right, right," screamed the capital city Board of Directors, nodding and clapping, nodding and clapping. "Tell us more," they shouted, nodding and clapping, clapping and nodding.

Dr. Swint, of GCCC, had just happened to be in city hall the day of the meeting to ask directions to the public library where he wished to do some scriptural research.

As he was asking the receptionist, the cheers of approval came from the meeting chamber. The Board had just approved the new names.

Dr. Swint had followed the noise and heard one of the Board members explain that nondescript names were best for a state virtually without history or heroes to commemorate.

Dr. Swint saw the wisdom of the Board position. So he went back to Gudge Creek Community College and talked the faculty committee-on-names out of anything pretentious. They, too, saw the wisdom of simplicity.

Police and fire protection in the towns of Gudge Creek (pop. 10) and Wad (pop. 9) have been satisfactory for years, perhaps owing to their simplicity and low cost.

Crime continues to be nonexistent. The towns do have a stoplight that could theoretically be run but never has been since it was put up a few years ago, prompted by a desire to be up-to-date communities.

A proposal to buy a used parking meter from the county seat was rejected. There still being only three cars in town, only two of which will run.

The fire protection is flawless since the hose at the DX station is now long enough to reach any building in either town.

What the towns lack is ambulance service. It was the subject of a recently called meeting of the Chambers of Commerce of the two towns, plus the Twin City Development Council.

The need for ambulance service is, of course, *pro forma.* Like the street light, it would serve little practical purpose. And from the beginning of local history, no one has ever been sick enough to be transported from one place to another.

Owing to the natural phenomenon that keeps the humidity constant and the temperature at seventy-two degrees—winter and summer—there has never been a record of even a common cold in either Gudge Creek or Wad, much less pneumonia or asthma. No one in either town smokes.

Still, in order to be eligible for a federal Reduction of Paperwork Grant, both towns were required to file forms listing ordinary municipal services that they were lacking.

Among those missing services was a city bus service. But even though federal funds were available to furnish a bus and a driver, the service was declined because, in Wad and Gudge

Creek, every building and dwelling is across the street from each other.

Wardell Vex, the executive director of the Twin City Development Council, had argued in favor of bus service but later admitted that such service would be practically useless since there was only room enough for one bus stop. It meant that passengers would get off where they got on.

But lack of ambulance service was something else. It was a clear need for the two cities. And the meeting of the Development Council decided that both towns could share just one ambulance service, along with its personnel.

"Now," said Vex, "clearly in the interests of free enterprise, we should hire a private ambulance service and let them charge what the traffic would bear."

Vex then introduced a consultant brought in from the state capital to explain what should be done.

"We propose a modest charge of only three hundred and fifty dollars to answer an emergency call," the consultant said, gesturing with a pointer toward a large poster with graphs on it.

"A bargain!" exclaimed Vex, beaming.

"Of course if the patient wanted to be carried on to the doctor, it would be *another* three hundred and fifty dollars." The consultant explained that was the going price for ambulance services in towns with populations under twenty.

"Well, I'll tell you one dang thing," broke in Uncle Dave Hicks. "I'll go to the doctor in a mule-and-wagon before I'll lay out a fare like *that!*"

Uncle Dave's declaration sent a fresh breeze through the room. It was voted to accept his gift of a flat-bed wagon and a fifteen-year-old mule to serve as the towns' ambulance service.

"It ain't but a hundred yards to ol' Doc Dawson's Veterinary Infirmary from any place in town."

The consultant was shown the door and everybody went home.

NEW ORLEANS' POLICE STRIKE THREATENS TO CANCEL
MARDI GRAS ESTIMATED $200 MILLION TO BE LOST
TO CITY'S COMMERCE, ACCORDING TO ESTIMATE

This recent headline was viewed equably by the city fathers of
the twin communities of Gudge Creek (pop. 10) and its adjoining bedroom community, Wad (pop. 9).

Wardell Vex, director of the Twin City Community Development Council, in sanguine spirit, fired off a letter to the
mayor of New Orleans explaining how Mardi Gras can be
saved, tourists bilked, and a good time had by all as usual.

"You can simply follow the Gudge Creek-Wad parade plan,"
Vex wrote to the mayor.

The wisdom of the plan is immediately apparent. Gudge
Creek and Wad are very civic minded, self-promoting communities, and ceremonial parades are held on many occasions during the year.

It was explained to the mayor how, since the two communities share only one street between them, and it is unpaved
and less than a block long, it was realized long ago that a moving parade was impractical, and how, on high days in the twin
cities, a wagon is dragged into place before the general store,
it is festively decorated as a float, the four-way loudspeaker is
switched on at the Second Baptist Church across the street,
and a martial record is put on the community Victrola. Then,
to the music of the "Marine Hymn" and "King Cotton" (the
only march record available), the townspeople strut around the
stationary float, ogling at it and admiring it from all sides.

On patriotic holidays, such as Independence Day, the float is
festooned with red-white-and-blue streamers. At the annual

Homecoming of Gudge Creek Community College, the wagon bed is draped in school colors, green and green, and the college basketball team (which is also its entire student body) mounts the float and waves as the proud townspeople cheer and applaud. "Sweet Georgia Brown" plays on the Victrola.

(Gudge Creek Community College enjoys a unique reciprocal agreement with Mineshaft Community College in Mineshaft, Pennsylvania. The team serves both schools as team and student body. This plan of sharing a student body between two colleges was necessitated by the growth of the community college system. There are so many tax-supported community colleges that there are simply not enough students to go around. The team is bused between the two schools.)

Mr. Vex, in his letter to the mayor, suggested that the Mardi Gras parades could be designed after the Gudge Creek–Wad parade plan, except on a much grander scale. The magnificent floats could be towed into position on Canal Street during the night. Then, at parade time the next day, the revelers would be turned loose from neighboring streets and allowed to pour out onto Canal Street and mill happily and excitedly about the floats. Bands would play but not march. They would simply mark time in their assigned positions.

Rex and his court, instead of passing by the revelers, would be passed by the moving throngs. Candy and favors can be hurled as easily from a stationary platform as from a moving float.

"Better to have a non-moving parade than no parade at all," Vex observed in his letter to the mayor.

As yet, no reply has been received.

While I've never been to New Orleans during the Mardi Gras and am ignorant of the joys of it, it does seem a shame to me that police and city officials have chosen this high season for such a disastrous standoff.

It would be better to wait for the gloomy deep purple days of Lent to sit down and negotiate. The atmosphere would be soberer, heads clearer, and crowds less volatile.

45

It seems sort of stick-in-the-muddish to appropriate such a gala festival to use as leverage in a labor dispute.

But, all that aside. Let New Orleans follow the Gudge Creek–Wad example. Those two towns didn't let the simple fact that they didn't have a street long enough for a parade keep them from having a parade. It just takes a little imagination to get around troublesome obstacles.

———————————

The board of Gudge Creek Community College took under advisement an order from the Sunflower Academic Accrediting Agency that all academic activity at the college cease owing to the inadequacy of the teaching plant and incompetence of the teaching staff.

"We are now trying to determine whether a college has to teach academic subjects in order to establish and maintain a football team," said the college Vice President Lurton Soames.

Private investors were trying to buy the entire Gudge Creek campus. "We need parking for the stadium," Soames said, "and the best place to put a parking lot is where the college is located."

"Private investors would be happy to put up an unmanned parking lot. Football fans arriving for the game would put five dollars into a numbered slot in order to park, but the College of Arts and Sciences has frankly done got to be a ball and chain to progress here at the college," Soames said.

Despite the cease and desist order from the accrediting agency, college officials have decided to proceed with a basic core curriculum.

"We need to keep the kids occupied while they're not sleeping or practicing football," Soames said.

The core curriculum will include:
* Applied Spelling 201, a survey through the letter "L"
* Penmanship 102, basic pencil printing, plus an introduction to the cursive alphabet
* Nutrition 214, use of the knife and fork
* Reading 111, understanding highway signs
* Hygiene, hair care with emphasis on the part
* Music, memorization of "Jesus Loves Me" and "God Bless America"

The board also voted against reconstructing the chemistry building, which was destroyed in an explosion of the still.

"It warn't nothing but a tin-roofed building nohow," Soames explained. He said the accident occurred when some sophomore students attempted without authorization to make a run of new spirits in preparation for the college prom that was to have been held the following week.

Uncle Dave Hicks, the town's resident bootlegger and professor of chemistry, maintains a modern plant outside of town. When he installed the new computerized distillery, he donated the old still to the college in memory of his grandmother.

Soames said that while the academic departments would be closed, college social life would be maintained along with the athletic programs.

"The kids can continue to drive around and drink beer," Soames said. "It's the stuff from which memories are made."

———————————

I ran into my old friend, State Representative Wallace Wad of Wad (pop. 9) in the cafeteria line the other day.

Both of us were alone, so I invited him to share a table with me, which he did. It was nice to be filled in on the happenings and events in the town of Wad and its twin city, Gudge Creek (pop. 10).

"You wouldn't think so much could get skewed around in such little towns," Representative Wad chuckled, when I asked how things were going.

It seems that a great internal problem has arisen at Gudge Creek Community College.

"There's a party in the college that wants to secede."

"Secede from *what?*" I asked.

"The College of Arts and Sciences wants to secede from the Athletic Department, of which it is a branch," explained Representative Wad.

I remarked at the oddity of the association.

"Well, since the whole student body is made up of the basketball team, there ain't a whole lot of emphasis put on reading and writing," said Representative Wad.

"That's what's got the Arts and Sciences faculty upset. They feel that it's wrong for them to have to try to squeeze in classes between basketball practices."

I asked why they didn't ask the president of the college to call the coach on the carpet.

"Because at GCCC, the coach is ahead of the president. He makes more, he's got more power, and he's got more clout."

"In fact," Representative Wad said, "the coach has threatened to fire the president if he don't quit spending school money on frills."

"Frills?" I said.

"Teaching aids and such. Books. Spellers."

He said that only last week the coach happened by while a truck was delivering a box of readers to the English department. "He threw a fit," Wad chuckled. "He went right in to the head of the English department and told her in no uncertain terms that the college budget didn't make any allowances for such trivia."

The shipment was refused, Representative Wad said. That's

when the faculty of the College of Arts and Sciences held their rebellion.

"But it won't come to nothing. To have a rebellion at a college you've got to have the student body on your side, and at GCCC, the entire student body is on the basketball team."

I remarked that it was quite unusual for the school budget to be controlled by the athletic department. Representative Wad was philosophical about it.

"They just don't make no bones about it. That's what the school's for—to play basketball. There's just some silly rules about college basketball and football teams having to be attached to real colleges," he said.

I asked if he thought the College of Arts and Sciences could go it alone.

Representative Wad shook his head. "If they pull out, they won't have nowhere to hold classes. They meet in the boiler room and janitor's storeroom of the gymnasium now. There's nowhere for them to go."

He said overtures had been made to the Second Baptist Church of Gudge Creek to use their parlor and Sunday School rooms. "But the preacher wanted them to promise to stop teaching about evolution as a condition."

Representative Wad poured his coffee into his saucer and lifted it to sip it neatly, in one gulp. He daintily wiped his lips.

"I swan," he said, "I just don't know where it's all a-gonna end."

Uncle Dave Hicks, the leading philanthropist and wealthiest man in the town of Gudge Creek (pop. 10), needs no instructions on the use of alcohol as automobile fuel.

Uncle Dave has been running his own truck for years on the spirituous product of his own factory, located on the banks of the creek from which the town took its name.

City dwellers will be surprised to learn that there is no difference between the alcoholic product that Uncle Dave sells for refreshment purposes (to a regular list of loyal customers), and the product on which he runs his truck.

Uncle Dave drove from Gudge Creek to the state Capitol the other day and, through the introduction of State Representative Wallace Wad of Wad (pop. 9), I conducted an informative interview with him.

I found him to be a wiry old man, elderly in years but youthful in outlook. His language was spicy, and the pink of his cheeks seemed the result of optimistic spirit, plus an occasional pull from a pewter flask.

"I call it my pacemaker," he said, and we all laughed. It was a vintage Uncle Dave-ism.

I asked the old gentleman how he managed to maintain an untaxed distillery without interruption from local authorities.

"*I'll* tell you how," Uncle Dave snapped. "I pay more contributions to anybody and everybody in them two cussed towns than I'd pay if my liquor was legal. If I was to close up, the whole county would be on welfare."

We all chuckled nervously.

"*I* ain't ashamed of it," he retorted to our reaction. "If I was to close up so would the Boy Scouts, the Gudge Creek Community College, the fire department, the high school. And the preacher'd have to go to work to support hisself."

Uncle Dave abruptly stopped his tirade and broke into laughter. "I even reroofed the jail in the county seat. And you know *what?* They named it the 'Dave Hicks Memorial Roof,' and I ain't even dead yet."

Uncle Dave continued his chuckling. "I figured that if ever the politicians got honest, they'd put me in it, and I'm too old to be uncomfortable."

The real purpose of our meeting was to discuss Uncle Dave's success at developing such a high quality brand of moonshine whiskey that it could be used without alteration in an internal combustion engine.

"Well, that ain't exactly right," answered Uncle Dave. "Either it's got to be diluted a little, or the truck motor's got to be geared down. When I first tried it in my truck, I couldn't keep it under fifty miles an hour in first gear. And *that* was going uphill.

"I finally got it under control by unplugging all but one of the spark plugs. And still it's a little too peppy for most people."

I asked the self-made scientist what he used to dilute the fuel with.

"Well, anything is better than nothing. I poured four gallons of buttermilk in the tank once. It don't make no difference. Tap water, Cokey Cola, *anything*."

Wouldn't some of those additives foul up the spark plugs?

"It's self cleaning. You can pour sorghum in the tank with that stuff and them plugs'll come out shining like a possum's eye in a high light beam."

He said that on his way to the capital city he had to run his truck in first or second gear to keep it within the fifty-five mile an hour speed limit. "I ain't got no idea how fast it would go if I opened it up."

The interview ended soon after that. It had been a pleasant experience for me. But Uncle Dave had signaled that he had had enough. He wanted to get started back home.

"The energy people invited me over here to tell them about my invention, but I decided not to talk to 'em. It scared me off when they said they could probably make me rich."

I was glad to run across my old friend, State Representative Wallace Wad of Wad, at the public library the other day.

He is back in town for the renewed session this week of the General Assembly, which he has served long enough to earn the chairmanship of the House Committee on Absentee Voting. The Committee is charged with punching the buttons on the electronic voting machines of members who, for one reason or another, are absent from the chamber during crucial votes.

"We'd have to close up the House if we had to depend upon all the members being present for every vote," he commented.

Representative Wad reported, upon questioning, a banner year of progress in his hometown of Wad (pop. 9) and its twin community, Gudge Creek (pop. 10). Indeed, it was plans for construction of library shelves at the Gudge Creek Community College that caused Representative Wad to be at the capital city public library where I met him.

"They ast me to check out a book to bring back home. They need to take some measurements to see how wide the shelves can be."

He said that a rich benefactor had bequeathed a set of *Reader's Digest* condensed books to the college, plus eighteen volumes of a twenty-volume set of *The Book of Knowledge* (1918 edition).

"We felt it was a gift of enough importance to provide adequate housing for it."

Representative Wad had already been in town a couple of days when I saw him. "We've had to have our housekeeping meetings out at the state house," he said. "I had my own committee work to look out for, and as I'm also vice chairman of the House Prayer Room Maintenance Committee, there was some preparation work to do." He said it mostly amounted to knocking down the dirt dobbers' nests. I asked him how his trip had been. "Jes' fine. I caught the tri-weekly pickup from home to the highway, and then rode to the city with the UPS man. Anyway, the bus don't run less it's got a full load, and sometimes it takes a spell to fill one up. They only made one trip last month."

I remarked that I thought UPS wouldn't take a parcel that weighed more than one hundred pounds. "They will if it can walk," he answered.

Representative Wad revealed the only inconvenience of being shipped by UPS. He said he had had himself addressed to the home of his landlady where he had rented a room for several years. "She wasn't home when we got there," he chuckled, "and the UPS man had to leave me with a neighbor."

The legislator and I strolled through the library stacks looking for the books we had come for. I was searching for a book on temperance, and Representative Wad was seeking a book that would be typical in size for a college library, one that would provide the design prototype for others that would eventually occupy the shelves of the new library.

"I'm not doing this chore with much enthusiasm," he said. "The college has so many greater needs than a liberry. I don't want to seem ungrateful for the gift, but the gift of books will change the whole complexion of the college's operation."

He said that inflation has taken its toll on the college, too, and that such essentials as a new basketball floor, scoreboard repairs, and a boost in the coach's salary needed to be fulfilled.

He reduced his choice of books to three as being of suitable size for the library. He rejected *On the Origin of Species* on moral grounds, although its size was nearly ideal. He liked the cover on *Do-It-Yourself Carburetor Repair,* but dropped it in favor of *Leaves of Gold,* which he thought his wife might like to thumb through before he turned it over to the college's architectural committee.

We both walked back to the checkout desk with our selections, shook hands on the sidewalk outside, and went our separate ways.

Basketball has always been the main sport of Gudge Creek Community College, especially as its team coincides exactly with the male student body, and vice versa. Academic classes at the college are scheduled between practice sessions.

And now, for the first time, the school's Board of Trustees authorized a football program. "We found," said Dr. Brewster Lurton, GCCC president, "that by streamlining our academic program we could save enough money to hire a coaching staff, as well as equip and train a prize-winning football team."

The move was widely hailed in coaching circles by many who had been alarmed at what they considered undue emphasis on teaching in American colleges.

Gudge Creek Community College realized an upsurge in student applications, while colleges in general had been experiencing a decline.

"We credit our advanced program of requiring a diploma for entrance to the college," Dr. Lurton said. "If you put a false emphasis on such educational esoterics as reading and writing, you miss a great many otherwise eligible football players."

He said Gudge Creek Community College offered *elective* courses in reading and writing so that any football player who wished to take them could do so between practice sessions.

The twin towns of Gudge Creek (pop. 10) and Wad (pop. 9) were elated at the new football program. Buildings in both towns sprung out in school colors (green and green—thanks to a generous gift to the college of a surplus string of pennants by the local DX service station).

And immediately, talk boosting a stadium began.

Wardell Vex, the director of Twin City Development Council, called a meeting to get plans afoot.

A fairly flat pasture behind Second Baptist Church has traditionally been used for outdoor games at Gudge Creek and Wad. The only extras that were needed for a football game (which is to say a ball and a sack of lime to draw the lines with) had been donated.

"But times are changing," explained Dr. Lurton at the meeting. "It's important for the players and for the winning of football games to have a large stadium."

As any planner will tell you, the size of a stadium is computed from the size of the communities in which they are located, plus the average numbers of expected visitors.

"Let's see," said Vex, putting a pencil to paper. "Gudge Creek has a population of *ten* (writing down the number) and Wad has *nine* (also noting the number and drawing a line under them). That makes—bring down the nine—that makes nineteen."

"Wait now, Wardell," broke in Mrs. Vernelle Inch. "Uncle Dave Hicks don't go to ball games. So you can't count him."

"Well, he'll count just as good as any of us when we apply for a feddle grant from the gov'ment."

"Well, I just hate to see us overbuild," Mrs. Inch lamented.

The expected number of "visiting" fans was quickly extrapolated and was put at fourteen.

"All right," said Vex, "If we don't count Uncle Dave Hicks, we'll have to build a stadium that will hold at least thirty-three people."

Dr. Lurton was on his feet. "We must think of future growth," he urged. "And anyway, the federal government won't look at such a small figure. I propose a stadium of at least 46,000 seats, plus press box and photo deck."

The room gasped. State Representative Wallace Wad of Wad rose slowly.

"Dr. Lurton," he began. "Even if we get the money, we ain't got enough of a flat spot to build anything that wide."

Dr. Lurton reminded the meeting that, as long as they were getting federal funds, they might as well think big. The meeting went long into the night. A report was expected by morning.

"What our two communities need," said Wardell Vex, speaking without notes, "is a football stadium."

Vex was addressing a special joint session of the Twin City Development Council, of which he is executive director, and the Gudge Creek–Wad Chamber of Commerce. His statement was greeted with hearty applause.

The entire faculty of Gudge Creek Community College had been invited to the meeting, and they joined in the hand-clapping, nodding and beaming among themselves.

"And," said Vex, "we need a *big* stadium, one that will hold lots of people, bands, and whatnot." (Applause. Vex had the crowd eating out of his hand.)

Stadium fever had taken over the twin towns, whose total population of nineteen could all fit on the front porch of the general store with room to spare. (This had actually happened once when a rainstorm blew up when the whole town had shown up to attend a parade.)

The attack of stadium fever had infected the town after the administration of Gudge Creek Community College altered entrance requirements to such an extent that a football program became possible. Students were no longer required to be able to read, write, or do addition of up to three numbers in order to matriculate. The new rules required matriculating students to know right from left (75 is passing) and which end of a pencil goes down.

These amendments caused a jump in enrollment and brought in enough boys to have both offensive and *dee*-fensive squads, with three or four left over. Enough girls enrolled to have cheerleaders.

The increased enrollment was also good for the academic end of the college. The mathematics department added an elective course in advanced subtraction, and the home economics department was able to institute a minor in biscuits.

Even though this is the first year for a football team at GCCC, and the team has yet to win a game, community support has been most enthusiastic, and talk of a stadium began immediately after the first game.

Games are presently played in a pasture behind Second Baptist Church. Football fans bring their own chairs and stools, making it possible for them always to have a seat on the line of scrimmage. A plank between two lard cans is provided for visiting spectators. Tickets are eight dollars and fifty cents, obtainable from the athletic department of GCCC, or at the gate. So far the plank has not been filled.

"Next season," continued Vex, "there will be a total of *four* home games. And while we couldn't hardly get a stadium built by then, it's a clear sign that we need to get started," (Applause.) "because by the next season, there'll be *five* home games. That's a—let's see—a twenty per cent increase, which indicates the dire need for adequate ath-a-letic facilities." (Applause.)

Vex went to an easel on which several large cards were placed. He removed the covering card to reveal a ground plan for a new stadium, and its relationship to the two towns. (Applause.) The plan showed that the northwest end of the proposed stadium would cover ground now occupied by Second Baptist Church, the DX station, and clear down to Uncle Dave Hicks's distillery on Gudge Creek.

"I be dammed, Fatso!" rumbled Uncle Dave, who was sitting in the back of the room. "You can take that grandstand and send her back where she come from."

"Now, wait, Uncle Dave," said Vex. "There's no need for alarm. This is gonna be a *big* stadium, and nothing's gonna have to be tore down to build it. There'll be plenty of room under the seats for your business, and for those other buildings. We plan just to build around you." Vex explained that the only relocation made necessary by the new structure would be moving the four-way loudspeakers to the other end of Second Baptist

Church. "It'd be a blessing if you'd move them devilish things outa the county," grumbled Uncle Dave, half to himself.

Vex went on to explain that federal matching funds, at a ratio of 500,000 to 1, were available for such projects. "To be eligible under Title VII, we'll have to build a stadium of 68,000 seats. And if we get started now, we'll have it ready for the football season year after next. (Applause.)

———————

State Representative Wallace Wad of Wad (pop. 9) looked uncommonly distinguished as he came out of the downtown Sterling Store wearing a new pair of glasses.

"These are 'twenty-sixes,'" Wad said, after he had given me a warm greeting. He had just arrived in town on the United Parcel Service truck to prepare for the special session of the State legislature which has been called by the governor.

"I just don't know where my other specs got to," he said. "I usually wear a size stronger, but they were temporarily out at Sterlings. It makes me feel good, like I'm not as old as I'm supposed to be."

Wad is now chairman of the House Committee on Absentee Voting. "Without these glasses I can't see what button to push when a representative is off the floor and can't do it for himself."

I asked Wad if it was strictly on the up and up for a member of the House to vote when he's absent.

"Oh, well," he said, playing down the answer, "we've got to know each other so well that we know how each other's going to vote. And just because a member can't attend a session shouldn't mean that he can't be recorded on an issue."

I asked Wad what he thought of the governor's calling a special session to put the check on rising utility rates.

"Well, he's a-trying to get re-elected. I'd a done the same thing, I guess," he said.

Does Wad think that power company rates are too high?

"Well, they just may be," he answered matter of factly, "but they don't bother us over in Wad and Gudge Creek."

"You see, we don't use no power from the power company," he said. "In fact, we are completely independent of *any* utility, including the telephone company."

I observed that I thought both Gudge Creek and Wad had electric service.

"Oh, yes," he answered, "we've got electricity. Running water, too. And our fuel has been taken care of into the next century."

He said the town has a Delco unit it ordered from Sears Roebuck years ago. It's been providing power to the two towns for at least two decades.

"Uncle Dave Hicks owns it," he said, "but he don't charge nobody nothing. We don't have no overhead lines. Everybody just runs extension cords from their houses to the Delco."

He said that they don't run it in the daytime, when it's light. "We really don't need it then." The single exception is on Sunday morning when it's turned on so Second Baptist Church can play their four-way loudspeakers before the church service.

"So, it don't make no difference to us whether the power company doubles or *triples* its rates." Wad said, adding, "But I'm going to try to find out what's best for the state and the people, and vote that way." Then he chuckled. "I'll tell you *one* danged thing. They's a bunch of scamps out there in that House. I never knew anybody could wheel and deal as much as some of them fellows do."

(Due to petrolacutation, their only need for fuel in Gudge Creek and Wad is for cooking, and that has been supplied in perpetuity by a derailment many years ago of a dozen Rock Island railroad cars loaded with coal. The pile up was near enough to the communities so that they could use the fuel that was accidentally delivered to their doorstep. Estimates say that at the present rate, there's still enough left to last the towns another fifty years or more.)

"Well, it was nice seeing you, Mr. Chubb," said Wad. "I need to hustle on out to the Capitol building and lay the groundwork."

It was nice to have seen Representative Wad. I always learn something new from him.

A glumness has settled over the athletic department of Gudge Creek Community College.

"We cain't win for losin'" assistant basketball coach Ludlow Lurton complained to his wife over breakfast.

"What's the matter, sweetheart?" she asked, pouring more coffee.

"Well, don't let this get out of the room, but too much education seems to be interfering with our team. Them boys is wastin' too much time goin' to class."

"I thought they were exempted from class attendance," said Mrs. Lurton.

"It'd make a better program if they were," said Lurton, shaking his head. "Unfortunately, a state law says anybody that's matriculated has to attend a class at least once a week, as long as it don't interfere with practice and road trips."

"Well, can't you work out a major for them that would require them to spend all their time in the gym?"

"We're working on it. In the meantime, we've eased the inconvenience as much as possible. Each player has his own Barcalounger in the back row. Coach likes 'em to stretch out as much as possible when they ain't practicing. We've also put up baskets on the outside of every building so they can shoot wherever they are on campus."

"Well, hon, I don't want nobody to suffer. But how do they pass enough courses to stay eligible when they don't hit a class but once a week?"

"Passing ain't the problem. We give them special tests designed by the National Coaches' Association. They are all multiple-choice, but with only one space to be checked. The curve is set so everybody makes a 3.2 average."

"That's not a bad grade point."

"Well, we try to prepare them for life after basketball."

"I didn't know there was such a thing," Mrs. Lurton chuckled.

"And did you know . . . some of them boys want to learn to read and write? We got one boy who's almost halfway through *McGuffey's Third Reader.*"

"My lands! There's some deep stuff in that. Ain't that a bit stiff for him?"

"A lot of times when he ain't playing, he'll be readin' the book a-sittin' on the bench."

"Lord! . . . Don't that hurt the morale of the rest of the team?"

"Well, Coach finally told him that if he wanted to stay in the program, he was going to have to start acting like a basketball player. Coach said it's bad for recruiting."

"What'd the boy do?"

"Well, we think he's doing things like reading in the bathroom and even with a flashlight under the covers after he goes to bed."

"Are you gonna let him stay on the team?"

"It's a problem."

Lurton drained his coffee and pushed away from the breakfast table.

"Well, have a good day at the gym," his wife said, pecking him on the cheek.

"I'll be chauffeuring Coach in his Cadillac over to the Twin City Optimist Club at noon today. He's gonna give a speech appealing for funds for the college liberry."

"They've always got their hand out," she snapped in disgust. "Ain't there no end to it?"

"Well, the liberry is trying to raise enough money to buy another volume to their World Book set. They're up through "J". They want to get up through "N" by next year, so they can offer a degree in Nuclear Physics."

"Well, you just tell that scamp that I said to remember what he's here for," Mrs. Lurton chuckled again.

The twin communities of Gudge Creek (pop. 10) and Wad (pop. 9) have been torn asunder in recent weeks over the question of whether to float a 22 million dollar bond issue to finance a giant convention center and sports arena.

The Gudge Creek–Wad Chamber of Commerce Ad Hoc Committee for the Convention Center and Sports Arena proposed that the only way to make such a complex successful was to build it in the center of town where traffic congestion is highest. Also, it was deemed important by the committee to put it in a place occupied by a successful business. The only successful business in either community is the general store in Gudge Creek. So it was decided, initially, that to make the complex successful, that the general store would have to be torn down and the center built in its place. The architect later revised the plan so that the convention center could be built *over* the general store. It would be tucked under the bleachers at one end.

These arguments have not gone unheeded by members of the community who must vote on the issue. But Gudge Creek and Wad are naturally towns with conservative natures, and they found that they must realistically examine the negative aspects.

The citizens cannot be accused of being nonprogressive. Indeed, they financed and built the Gudge Creek Community College, hired a faculty to lecture in arithmetic and remedial reading, and then went out and recruited the entire student body from Mineshaft, Pennsylvania. Fortunately, the entire student body made up the basketball team which has brought fame to the two small communities. Later, a music department was formed in the college when a church gave them a piano.

But 22 million dollars is a big figure, and when the two towns vote on the bond issue later this month the citizenry must weigh the advantages which a large convention and sports complex would bring to a community of nineteen people against the disadvantages of the giant debt.

Wardell Vex, a Chamber of Commerce official and director of Twin City Development Council, is strongly in favor of the complex. In a presentation given a joint meeting of the city councils of the communities, he pointed out that he has already received a commitment for the state convention of the Cowbell Manufacturers Association, and that the likelihood "looks good" for a regional meeting of Organic Fertilizer Dealers and their woman's auxiliary, the Organic-Annes.

Vex has been convincing, and his eloquent persuasion will be a principal factor *if* the bond issue carries in the coming election.

An outspoken opponent is Mrs. Foster Cue, the operator of the Boat Dock Cafe, who argues that for that amount of money the twin communities could build an international airport, finance a municipal transit system forever, support a symphony orchestra, pave the main street (it has never been paved and it has never been named), and put up a water tank.

Mrs. Cue has also been persuasive, and if the bond issue is defeated she will be able to take much of the credit. She also opposes the complex for personal reasons. If the general store in Gudge Creek would be incorporated into the center under the eastern bleachers, Mrs. Cue's Boat Dock Cafe, which is located on Gudge Creek, would find itself just off the lower floor men's room of the sports arena.

Gudge Creek and Wad have known turmoil before, and they

have always comported themselves well while under stress. The most recent controversy was a proposal by the Power and Light Company to build a new coal-fired steam generating plant on the banks of Gudge Creek. The plans were later abandoned after ecology groups complained, but if it had been built it would have required some readjustment which the communities were not willing to make. Both towns would have been under the plant's coal pile.

The outcome of the election will be revealed in later reports.

———————

One of the many advantages of living in the twin towns of Gudge Creek (pop. 10) and Wad (pop. 9) is poor television reception and irregular newspaper delivery.

"It means," declared Uncle Dave Hicks speaking to the annual Gudge Creek–Wad Chamber of Commerce banquet, "that we don't get broadcasts of panhandling TV evangelists, and by the time the newspapers get here, the bad news is so old it's too late to worry about it."

Living in a secluded mountain valley, off the main paved roads, has given Wad and Gudge Creek residents an enviable lifestyle, he advised his audience.

The Chamber's spring banquet, in the parlor of Second Baptist Church, is one of the social highlights of the year, with full attendance by townspeople.

"The only money that changes hands in the name of religion in Wad and Gudge Creek," said Uncle Dave, "is what's dropped into the plate here every Sunday morning. It stays here for our own missionary work. It don't get sent out of town to some slick-haired television preacher so he can get Jacuzzi jets put in his baptismal tank."

Uncle Dave waxed warm to one of his favorite subjects.

"You can look at some of these TV preachers and tell they spend more on hair oil and pomade than they do on soap.

"And when that Baton Rouge preacher laid out fifty dollars for fun and games in a New Orleans motel, what widder woman was it that sent him that fifty dollars in the first place? We can be thankful that it didn't come out of our pockets here in the twin cities because, by the grace of God, we ain't got cable television."

Uncle Dave, distinguished professor of chemistry at Gudge Creek Community College, is also the biggest benefactor of Second Baptist Church. Any shortfall in tithes is made up for by a check from Uncle Dave who, as a result, has been chairman of the board of deacons beyond the memory of most church members.

This idyllic situation enjoyed by Wad and Gudge Creek is reviewed every spring at the Chamber of Commerce banquet, just in case somebody gets the idea of changing the delicate balance of what some consider the most blessed spot to live in in the state.

Uncle Dave is always the banquet speaker, and he invariably sets the tone that real progress is a fragile gift that promotes happiness, but not necessarily wealth and growth.

Uncle Dave reminded them that progress can as well come from not having something as having it. The towns, for example, have no lawyer, doctor, nor newspaper. As a result, they have lived in unalloyed peace and tranquility, and not a little prosperity.

"We don't have disputes big enough to support a law practice. And, anyway, when you get a lawyer, disputes get bigger than they need to be.

"We had a doctor once, and it seemed like a good idea. But there's so little stress in Wad and Gudge Creek, nobody smokes, and everybody eats fresh vegetables, that the doctor went bankrupt.

"We ain't really big enough to have a newspaper. With only nineteen people in town, everybody knows everything as soon as it happens, if they don't oversleep. And it ain't hard to catch up if they do.

"And we had a postoffice once, but we found out that mail got in and out of town quicker without it."

Uncle Dave outlined again some of those unique points that make life so livable in Wad and Gudge Creek.

"We ain't got a street long enough or flat enough to jog on. That keeps the town neater and prettier.

"And, owing to petrolacutation, our temperature never varies from seventy-two degrees, day and night, winter and summer.

"We got what we want," he concluded, "Now let's not mess with it."

Uncle Dave got a standing ovation from the townspeople, as usual.

Uncle Dave Hicks looked mad as he walked in through the doors of the Gudge Creek municipal court.

"I don't need no lawyer," snorted Uncle Dave when the acting municipal judge, Mrs. Vernelle Inch, asked him if he was represented.

"I know what I want to say, and I intend to get it said, and I don't need no high-priced county seat shyster saying it for me!"

Judge Mrs. Inch knocked a paperweight on the table to call for order so the proceedings could begin.

It seems that Uncle Dave was suing the Second Baptist Church, contending that the four-way rooftop loudspeakers that played between Sunday School and church every Sunday were too loud and constituted a nuisance.

"That racket is making my mash separate," Uncle Dave complained. "I ain't had a real good run from my still since they installed that thing."

Uncle Dave's distillery over on the banks of Gudge Creek is the handsomest and largest building in town. That it is unlicensed is a well-known and widely overlooked fact. Uncle Dave, who paid for the new roof on the jail at the county seat, remarked that he wanted to be comfortable in case the voters ever elected a new prosecuting attorney. And he is the biggest tither at the church he is suing.

"Are you sure that it's the sound volume that's causing the mash to separate in the kegs, Uncle Dave?" Judge Mrs. Inch asked.

"Well, Vernelle, it's either the loud noise, or the Anita Bryant record that they keep playing. But it don't make no difference which. The trouble comes out of them devilish speakers, whether it's the sound or the sentiment."

Judge Mrs. Inch scribbled notes.

(It should be mentioned that the municipal Court of Gudge Creek and its neighboring town of Wad is informal, without any direct roots back to the state constitution. But the citizens have found it cheaper to run it the way they do, rather than let paid judges and lawyers run it.)

"It ain't the loudness of the speakers that saves the souls," Uncle Dave observed. "But them deacons over there has got the idea that the longer the radius of the gospel songs, the more sinners will be brought to the bar."

Uncle Dave said the needle got stuck in a Tennessee Ernie Ford gospel song one Sunday and it cut the proof of his entire warehouse by more than half. "That ain't right," Uncle Dave said.

"Well, Dave," said Mrs. Inch, "exactly what are you asking for?"

"Vernelle, I wish they'd take that dang thing off the roof and drop it in Gudge Creek. This used to be a quiet neighborhood."

Judge Mrs. Inch nodded.

"But all I've got a right to ask," continued Uncle Dave, "is that they turn them speakers down enough so that they don't ruin my business."

The courtroom, though packed, was quiet.

"Whiskey takes quiet and tranquility to make," Uncle Dave explained. "And man don't make whiskey. Al-kee-hawl forms by the unchangeable laws of nature when yeast acts on sugars. That's the way it always has been, and always will be. So, it stands to reason that anything that man does to upset the laws of nature must be bad."

In Heaven, Aristotle shook hands with St. Thomas Aquinas. Applause swept the courtroom as Uncle Dave sat down.

Judge Mrs. Inch knocked on the table with the paperweight to signal she wanted to speak.

"All right, Dave, I'll rule in your favor. Thurston, run over to the preacher's study and tell him to turn down their speakers so they can't be heard no farther than the DX station across the street. There ain't no point in making a federal case out of anything that a little good will can tend to."

The end of the spring semester brought some soul-searching at Gudge Creek Community College.

"Not a single member of the basketball team earned a single credit hour during the spring semester," moaned Brewster Lurton, college president. "Not one!"

Coach Fabius Still scraped his feet on the rug. "Brewster, I know there have been a few shortcomings. But don't judge the boys too harshly."

"Leave the judgments to me, Coach. Now I want to talk to each and every one of the boys by theirselves."

"They's waiting just outside. I'll get the first one."

A hulking six-foot-eight beanpole with knuckles hanging just below his knees dodged the door sill and entered the room.

"Name?" asked the president, holding pencil to paper.

(Scratching his knee.) "Sarcophagus Jones."

"Spell your first name."

"B."

"B? Sarcophagus doesn't start with B."

"It don't?"

"It starts with S."

"That's what I meant. Sometimes they look alike when they are wrote out."

"Second letter?"

"J."

"There's no J in Sarcophagus."

"I can't spell Sarcophagus. I was working on my second name."

"Okay. J-O-N-E-S. Is that right?"

"That sounds about right."

"Well, is it right or wrong?"

"Well, if it's wrong, it ain't very wrong."

"Coach," snapped the president, "has it occurred to you that this boy can't read or write?"

"Well, sir. I never paid no mind to it. He throws the ball good without readin'. And he made all A's in make-up summer school last summer at the University of Festus, Sunflower Branch."

"What did you study, Sarcophagus?"

"Er . . ." (looks at coach).

"Dr. Lurton, he taken 'History of Basketball since 1985,' 'Dribbling Through the Ages,' and a seminar on 'Why the Basketball is Round,' and 'Advanced Calculus.'"

"You took calculus, Sarcophagus?"

"I can read it, but I can't speak it yet."

"Coach Still, I think this college's basketball program is despicable!"

"Thank you, sir. It's nice to hear words of praise. We have tried to provide an ethical background for our boys in which learning and athletics go hand in hand."

A huge Air Force helicopter dropped from the skies on the outskirts of the twin towns of Gudge Creek (pop. 10) and Wad (pop. 9).

As the rotor whined down, two officers jumped to earth and scampered across the pasture toward the DX station. A contingent of men threw a cordon around the chopper to keep back an expected crowd. But in towns where the total population is only nineteen, no crowd materialized.

The only greeting committee was Uncle Dave Hicks, owner of the pasture, who gave the Air Force five minutes to get off his land.

Wardell Vex, executive director of the Twin City Development Council, was expecting the visit. He had arranged a meeting for the officers with the council at Gudge Creek Town Hall, and the meeting began as soon as the officers were shown into the room.

Vex introduced everybody to everybody else, and the meeting began.

"This is Major Truman Nerdlinger and Captain Felton D. Foscue, who has kinfolk in Gudge Creek. They will take turns in telling us what's on their minds."

"Greetings," said Major Nerdlinger after a patter of applause. "Contingent configurations relating to overweening military hardware commitments following an unprogrammed destruct, non-safetywise, of subterranean government retaliatory ballistic property, with concomitant evacuation of the resident populace, plus military . . ."

The major droned on for a couple of minutes and then nodded to the captain.

"Thank you, ladies and gentlemen," began the captain. "Major Nerdlinger was sent to give you the exact military terminology for our request. I'm here to translate into English what he has said."

The congregation sighed and shuffled around for comfort.

"As you know from the papers, the Air Force just destroyed one of its Titan II missiles. We are here to ask if we can install a replacement here at Gudge Creek and Wad."

"I'll be gol-danged if you will!" erupted Uncle Dave Hicks. (Uncle Dave had arrived a few minutes late, detained while he ran the Air Force helicopter off his property.)

Uncle Dave had long fought official encroachment. He led the battle against an effort by the state power company to put a coal-fired generating plant astraddle Gudge Creek. It had been sold to the citizens as a great boon to the two towns, requiring only a few adjustments. Like total relocation of both towns to make way for the coal pile, the evaporation of all the water in Gudge Creek, and the total devastation of the fishing industry.

"So you can just take your rockets and * * *."

"Now, Dave," said Vex, "let's let these men have their say."

"Let's run 'em out of town while the runnin's *good!*" retorted Hicks. "I used to think the worse thing that could happen to this town would be for a lawyer to move in. That ain't right. The *worse* possible thing that could happen would be to let the professional military get a toe in. We'd never be able to call anything our own again. And, not only that, we'd stand a chance of getting both our towns—and the whole county—blowed up. It looks like the military has got more weapons right *now* than they can handle."

"Good *peee*-ple." It was Major Nerdlinger, speaking sweetly. "You don't seem to collate correctly the catalyzing beta-situations made necessary by oscillized routine functions."

Captain Foscue wasn't listening. He was busy in conversation in the corner with state Representative Wallace Wad of Wad, Mrs. Foster Cue, who runs the Boat Dock Cafe, and others from the communities.

That's where the meeting actually ended. The two officers left. Major Nerdlinger, known to his colleagues as "Silver Tongue," would go on to become head of the United States Air Force. Captain Foscue would retire from the Air Force as soon as possible and move to Gudge Creek where he would head the Twin City Development Council's Anti-Military Committee.

————————————

The big event of the season in the twin communities of Gudge Creek (pop. 10) and its sister community, Wad (pop. 9), is the annual commencement exercises at Gudge Creek Community College.

The college is one of several that sprang up in the state at approximately the same time a few years ago, adding immeasurably to the cultural fabric of the community, and providing a useful way to use up surplus state education funds.

Since Gudge Creek became an education center, annual spring commencement exercises have become the high point of the year, marked by musical events, readings, and spellings.

The latter category, spellings, was added so that candidates for degree who were not far enough advanced to participate in readings (a graduate program) could show off for their parents.

Commencement exercises, of necessity, departed slightly from the norm; there was no one eligible to graduate from the college. But school officials felt that a lack of graduates was no reason not to have commencement activities as usual. And town as well as gown had come to expect, and look forward to, the annual festivities. Indeed, a delegation from both towns traditionally joined with college officials in meeting the baccalaureate speaker's bus.

That year's commencement address was given by the Assistant County Agent for Anthrax from the county seat, who was awarded an honorary Doctor of Philosophy degree and bus fare.

The baccalaureate sermon was delivered at Gudge Creek's Second Baptist Church by Little Pearl, a nine-year-old girl evangelist who has the reputation of being able to cure migraine headaches and break addicts of the Dentyne habit. The sermon had been scheduled to be held in her air-conditioned tent, but the truck was unable to negotiate the ruts leading down the hill into town.

There are few prouder moments in life than when a graduate steps up to receive his degree and a handshake from the president or vice-chancellor of the college. Even though there were no eligible graduates that year, the president of the college distributed rolled up sheets of blank paper to all those who had at least a 0.8 grade average, as a way of singling out achievement.

Music for all commencement functions is furnished by the college music department, which was founded after the Methodist Church in the county seat bought an electric organ and donated its old upright Mason and Hamlin to the college. The music department's library came into existence when a Broadman Hymnal was discovered in the piano bench. Appropriate music is directed by the wife of the president of the college who is head of the music department. She graduated *magna cum laude* in voice from the LaVerne College of Correspondence Careers, Chillicothe, Ohio.

The two towns of Gudge Creek and Wad join the college in celebrating spring commencement by staging a spectacular, but motionless, parade and festooning the sign at the DX station with strings of green-on-green pennants generously furnished by the company. The aforementioned float stands in front of the general store as spectators walk past it and the Victrola in the parlor of the Baptist Church plays the "Marines Hymn" through the four-way loudspeaker on the roof. It is a much anticipated occasion, especially loved by the children of the town.

Persons who have never known the civilized pleasures attendant upon a college commencement would do well to drive to Gudge Creek in the spring to observe the occasion.

Scene: Special called meeting of the Gudge Creek–Wad Chamber of Commerce Ad Hoc Committee for the Proposed Convention Center and Sports Arena. It's the day after the devastating defeat of a 22 million dollar bond election that the twin towns of Gudge Creek (pop. 10) and Wad (pop. 9) had called. The final vote, with one out of one precinct reporting, was: for, 2; against, 31.

Wardell Vex, committee chairman: Whew!

Mrs. Vernelle Inch, committee member: What now?

State Representative Wallace Wad, another committee member: We musta done something wrong.

Vex: Well, the voters just weren't in the mood for a 22 million dollar bond issue.

Mrs. Inch: I'll say! We only carried this committee by two-thirds.

Wad: Well, it's kindly a pity. The bond and real estate business in this township has been slumped for a long time, and this would have been a good way to help them fellers out.

Vex: I think what defeated it was that the new complex would have been built over the whole town. The general store would be under the east bleachers, and the Wad boat dock would have been near the first floor men's room.

Mrs. Inch: Then, too, it would have created a parking problem.

(The combined towns now have a total of four motor vehicles, three of which will now run, and as there is only the one short street in town, pollsters estimated that the parking question would be important in the minds of voters.)

Wad: Traffic is congested as it is, and we'd have had to hire off-duty policemen to direct traffic in the event of any convention that was hired to come here.

(The term "hire" was not entirely misused. Had the bond issue passed, part of the proceeds would have been paid to organizations to place their conventions in the twin cities.)

Mrs. Inch: There's a silver lining to every cloud. We'll just have to make better plans next time. Now it's time to get down to business and make do with what we have.

Vex: Well, as long as this Committee is in existence we might as well go ahead and adopt another project. Anybody got any ideas as to our priority of needs?

Mrs. Inch: We need to pave our street.

Vex: Now, Vernelle, let's don't be so provincial in our thinking. If outsiders hear we're letting a paving contract, everybody will think we're a hick town. Would you like to hear my proposal?

Wad and Mrs. Inch: Why, yes, Wardell. What do you propose?

Vex: I propose we propose a smaller bond issue to put in another electric traffic light.

Mrs. Inch: Another traffic light? Wardell, we don't even have an intersection.

Vex: Well, it'll certainly look better to outsiders if we put in traffic signals than if we pave a street. And we'll let the contract read "an *extension* of the traffic signal system."

Wad: That's gutsy thinking, Wardell, but with only four cars in town and some of *them* broke, we don't need a whole lot of control.

Vex: But we *do* need to look to the future. One day we'll have, maybe, ten cars. Or even a dozen. We might as well prepare for it now.

Wad: Do you think the town generator will stand the additional load?

Vex: It can if we turn out the lights in the public library when they ain't in use, which is most of the time.

Wad: Well, let's get on it. Progress don't visit the idle.

Mrs. Inch: Don't fret, Wardell. We'll have bulb salesmen beating a path to our door.

Summer is a-comin' in . . .

The scholars at Gudge Creek Community College already are packing their duds and pennants in preparation for returning home for the summer vacations.

The classrooms at Gudge Creek Community College will not be vacant for long. Indeed, they will be filled, after only a few days, with a branch of the Governor's School, an organization in which exceptional students from all over the state are to be exposed to upper level educational opportunities.

The school will be directed by professional educators but will reflect the governor's personal views on approximately everything.

Nominations of the faculty are now in progress, with the governor himself giving the final approval or veto.

Listed below are those educators who have been nominated—with their acceptance or rejection by the governor noted following their names.

* Kittredge J. V. Fenton-Soames, LLD, DD, DCL, OBE, VC: Warden of St. Regis College, Oxford; noted for his translation from Hebrew to Sanskrit of a history of the Essenes; winner of the Nobel Prize for his Shakespeare commentaries; rejected for the Governor's School as a "foreigner with ideas not acceptable for airing in the Governor's School."

* Lilburn Boochee: Barbed wire straightener of Rosehip; accepted as instructor of Advanced Architecture 1108A (Construction of Brush Arbors).

* Dame Edith Forben-Quill: Noted art historian; biographer of Titian; author of *The Nude in Renaissance Art*; rejected for "obvious reasons . . ."

* Zeldon Fraskle: Auto mechanic of Baseline Road Car and

Truck Clinic; accepted as lecturer on "The Philosophy of the Hub Cap."

* Sister Rosetta Pitts: Self-taught gospel pianist; author of *Jesus Couldn't Read Music*; accepted as professor of music. (Sister Rosetta, who can play Elgar's *Pomp and Circumstance* by ear, is much in demand for high school graduation ceremonies.)

* Jean-Claude Champollion: Descendent of the translator of hieroglyphs on the Rosetta Stone; professor of archaeology at the University of St. Jean-Paris; accepted *conditionally* with the provision that his lectures are to be monitored by a representative of the Teen-age Vigilante Committee to make sure that he does not let humanistic influences creep into his talks. (M. Champollion laughingly was told that he was to "reflect the governor's ideas" or he might be "hit by a load of bricks.")

* Dr. Sigismund Langsam-Fierlich: Greatest living authority of the works of Freud, Jung, and Sartre; rejected without comment. (Aides discovered the nomination form torn up in several pieces and cast into a cuspidor.)

* Dr. Merton Teasley: Professor of remedial shorthand at Sunscald Community College; accepted as professor of rhetoric and composition.

* Sultana Semmes: Dietician emeritus of Mudfork Retirement Home; compiler of *Sunset Collection of Toothsome Recipes for the Banana*; accepted as author in residence.

The selection process is continuing. It is reckoned to be a very difficult task, assuring that the intellectual cream of the state's youth is not subject to alien ideas and thoughts that are not up to normal standards accepted in the state.

Meanwhile, the Governor's School Film Selection Commission is finishing up its work. It had been admonished from upper echelons to reject any "X" or "R" rated rilms, any with alien humanistic themes, and any obvious garbage.

Films already approved by the Commission include: *Bambi and the Butterfly, Fantasia, Gone With the Wind* (with Rhett Butler's profanity changed to "darn!"), and *Ma and Pa Kettle Go to a Banana Republic.*

Classes and activities at Gudge Creek Community College are in full swing again and, except for minor problems in the athletic department, the school appears to be headed into its most successful year.

So the faculty was told at a meeting called by President Brewster Lurton. "Our enrollment is at its highest," Lurton announced. "Our library has been enlarged. And our basketball team is off to a 'hot' start."

Lurton indulged in the unaccustomed colloquialism to emphasize the administration's enthusiasm for the college team.

Faculty members were not as effervescent.

"The reason enrollment is so high," whispered Dr. Vanelda Davenport, head of the English Department, to a colleague, "is that nobody graduated last year."

"Too," Lurton went on, "we are expecting more out of our athletic teams this year, thanks to a readjustment of their academic schedule. We think our new procedures will be more humane for players trying to maintain a suitable average while so frequently traveling out of town."

The GCCC basketball team, it is true, has room for improvement. They had ended their last season with a win-loss record of 4–90. It had been a slight embarrassment to the administration and especially to Coach Fabius Still. The athletic budget is bigger than all other school budgets combined.

Before the schedule shift, the basketball team's only required academic course was Sunday School, taught by members of the coaching staff. Under the new curriculum required attendance at Sunday School was being dropped in favor of individual tutoring of team members. Each would be read a Bible story at bedtime by an assistant coach.

"We are particularly proud of improvements in our library," President Lurton asserted, "and I'm going to ask our acting librarian to give us a rundown on the upgrading."

Most of the time, the college library was kept in a pasteboard box under the basement stairs. It includes the first three volumes of the World Book, nine *Reader's Digest* condensed books, some back numbers of the *National Geographic* magazine, and a 1918 edition of the *Book of Knowledge.*

"Just this month," began acting librarian Burton Lull, "we have been bequeathed a complete set of the 'The World's Greatest Orations from Cicero to Patrick Henry,' 'The Practical Guide to Raising Angora Goats,' and a subscription to *Dry Cleaning Technology.*

"We feel that these will help fill some of the 'holes' we have in our book collection and enable the students to be more in touch with the wisdom of the ages."

"How many books were checked out last semester?" Dr. Davenport asked.

"Well, actually they was none actually checked out. Mrs. Lindsey's history class looked up the atomic bomb in the World Book." (Nods of satisfaction.) "So, you can see that the library has been a valuable asset to the school."

"Thank you, Burton," Lurton said. "Now that the positive and constructive news has been shared, let us turn to some of our minor problems."

Lurton outlined the shortcomings in the athletic department and how the school stood in danger of losing its standing in the Community College Athletic Association if additional funds weren't made available for the salary of coaches and for new athletic equipment.

"Hold it!" Dr. Davenport broke in. "The athletic department already spends more a year on witch hazel than the English department spends on teaching aids."

An embarrassing silence held the room a few seconds.

"Now, if we can pull ourselves together," Lurton said, "I think we can get on with the discussion. In order to meet the

budgetary needs of the athletic department for the next two se-
mesters, Coach Still has suggested certain economies in Arts
and Sciences. Coach Still?"

———————————

A couple from Milan, Georgia, has written asking for directions on how to get to Gudge Creek and Wad.

They read about the two communities in the paper while they
were visiting the state.

The towns seemed "very interesting' from the description,
they said, but "we have searched road maps for these towns . . ."
and "have failed to find them."

The letter, of course, was routed to me, and I am planning to
send the couple a note explaining how to go about inquiring
about a visit.

Admittedly, Wad and Gudge Creek are hard to find. I have
received a number of inquiries from around the state—and out
of state—from persons who are attracted to Gudge Creek and
Wad through curiosity, or because of the lovely living conditions that prevail there.

As a service to the communities, though, I don't print their
exact locations. They are small by choice, and are interested in
keeping it that way. Gudge Creek has a population of ten, Wad
of nine. There's a seasonal variation in the population of Gudge
Creek when the student body of Gudge Creek Community College reports for classes.

Both towns have been left off the official map of the Highway
and Transportation Department. Whether this is by design or
accident, I am not able to tell. But it has caused confusion and
some consternation. On one occasion, after we had printed an

explanation of petrolacutation, a representative of the Corps of Engineers called for directions.

Previously, a representative from the State Baptist Convention—who said he had "been through there" but couldn't remember where it was—called and asked to be reminded on how to get there. I satisfied his curiosity.

On a number of occasions, persons have called for directions. A man who had lived in Alaska during military service and was looking for a place to retire told me he needed help to find the towns.

And a representative from a senior citizens group that wanted to make a weekend excursion by bus asked for directions and if there was a place the passengers could eat at least one meal.

It's my policy not to give information as to the location of the towns over the telephone. The towns are not easy to find since they are slightly off the highway that runs to the county seat.

But, believe me, all letters are forwarded to the Twin City Development Council. There they are screened, and those from persons considered desirable are *perhaps* answered. Perhaps not.

"We've got it pretty much the way we want it," Wardell Vex, executive director of the Council, said. "So we are careful about whom we let in."

So, it's easy to see why newcomers are not welcome. And while visitors are allowed, they are voluntarily kept to a minimum of two. Each family who has, say, an aunt and a cousin who want to pay a visit, signs up at city hall. It means town facilities are never overcrowded with tourists.

I am writing the Georgia couple to explain that I'm forwarding their letter to the Twin City Development Council. If they are deemed desirable, they can perhaps expect a reply.